Essential
Portugal

AAA Publishing 1000 AAA Drive, Heathrow, Florida 32746

Portugal: Regions and Best places to see

 Best places to see 34–55 Featured sight

 Porto and the North 81–112 Évora and the Alentejo 143–164

 Lisbon and Central Portugal 113–142 Faro and the Algarve 165–185

Original text by Martin Symington

Updated by Apostrophe S

American editor: G.K. Sharman

Edited, designed and produced by AA Publishing
© Automobile Association Developments Limited 2008
Maps © Automobile Association Developments Limited 2008

978-1-59508-223-7

Published in the United States by AAA Publishing,
1000 AAA Drive, Heathrow, Florida 32746
Published in the United Kingdom by AA Publishing

Color separation: MRM Graphics Ltd
Printed and bound in Italy by Printer Trento S.r.l.

A03567
Maps in this title produced from mapping © MAIRDUMONT / Falk Verlag 2007
Transport map © Communicarta Ltd, UK

About this book

This book is divided into five sections.

The essence of Portugal pages 6–19
Introduction; Features; Food and Drink; Short Break including the 10 Essentials

Planning pages 20–33
Before You Go; Getting There; Getting Around; Being There

Best places to see pages 34–55
The unmissable highlights of any visit to Portugal

Best things to do pages 56–77
Good places to have lunch; top activities; best beaches; places to take the children; golf courses; peace and quiet and more

Exploring pages 78–185
The best places to visit in Portugal, organized by area

Maps
All map references are to the maps on the covers. For example, Tavira has the reference 🟥 11Y – indicating the grid square in which it is to be found

Admission prices
Inexpensive (under €4)
Moderate (€4–€10)
Expensive (over €10)

Hotel prices
Price per room per night:
€ budget (under €70);
€€ moderate (€70–€120);
€€€ expensive (over €120)

Restaurant prices
Price for a three-course meal per person without drinks:
€ budget (under €15);
€€ moderate (€15–€30);
€€€ expensive (over €30)

Contents

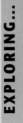

The essence of...

Portugal is the last remaining relatively undiscovered country of Western Europe. Those with enough time on their hands to travel from one end to the other will discover a staggering variety of scenery, architecture and ways of life.

They will also find a country whose national character has been shaped by history, geography and centuries of warfare with Spain, Portugal's great Iberian rival. Portugal looks out to sea. Cut off from the rest of Europe, it has always had to do so. This explains why such a small nation became one of the great seafaring countries of the world.

Today, Portugal is a modern state and a member of the European Union, but the visitor need not dig very deep to find more ancient traditions.

features

Millions of holidaymakers have visited Portugal over the last thirty years. The great majority of them have been lured to the Algarve by the south coast's sandy coves, manicured golf links, gaily painted fishing boats and lively nightlife in the busy resorts; few are disappointed. Others explore the great cities of Porto and Lisbon, or seek out the swinging resorts of Estoril and Cascais on the Lisbon coast.

The real joy of travelling in Portugal is that it is still one of the least discovered corners of Western Europe. A feeling of isolation still permeates the character of this nation of about 10 million souls out on the southwest extremity of the continent.

GEOGRAPHY

Portugal lies at the southwest extremity of continental Europe, forming the western edge of the Iberian peninsula. The country's only neighbour is Spain, with whom the River Minho forms a natural border in the north. Eastwards a backbone of craggy mountains divides the old adversaries, while expansive plains stretch down to the sea.

CLIMATE

The Algarve enjoys a Mediterranean-type climate with long hot summers, mild winters and more

than 3,000 hours of sunshine a year, although there is always a possibility of rain between September and May.

In the Alentejo, the hinterland of the Beiras and the Alto Douro, summers can be searingly hot. Spring and autumn are cooler, with winters in the mountain regions getting very cold with sub-zero temperatures and snow in the Serra da Estrela.

Porto and the Minho enjoy a temperate climate, with cooler temperatures year round, and the strong possibility of rain any time between autumn and spring.

POPULATION

The current population is about 10 million, although around 3 million more Portuguese live as migrant workers in France, Germany, the USA, Canada, Venezuela and elsewhere.

LANGUAGE

The national language is Portuguese. In written form, it appears similar to Spanish, but the sound is much more guttural, making it generally more difficult for foreigners to learn and understand.

RELIGION

About 99 per cent of the Portuguese population is Roman Catholic. There are small Protestant and Jewish communities.

food & drink

A traditional Portuguese meal is a big, lusty affair involving several courses.

There are many regional variations and specialities. However, there is one food in particular which unites the national palate – *bacalhau*, or dried, salted cod. There are many ways of preparing it, such as *Gomes de Sá* (in layers with diced potatoes, onions, olives and hard-boiled egg); and *Conde de Guarda* (creamed with mashed potatoes and cabbage).

Many Portuguese meals begin with a bowl of steaming soup. One to look for is *caldo verde* – cabbage shredded finely and flavoured with garlic sausage.

Fish and seafood are also much favoured and abundantly available, particularly in coastal towns. *Camarões* (shrimp), *gambas* (prawns), *sapateira* (giant, hairy crab) and *lagosta* (lobster), all caught in the cold, deep Atlantic, are wonderful and very pricey. Among the best fresh fish are *espada* (scabbard fish), *carapau* (horse mackerel), *linguado* (sole), and of course the ubiquitous *sardinhas* (sardines). *Pescada* (hake) can be good, too, but make sure it is *fresca* (fresh) not *congelada* (frozen).

The meat dishes in Portugal may be presented as a casserole or grilled on a skewer, be it *bife* (steak), *porco* (pork), *frango* (chicken) or *cabrito* (goat). In the north, stew is often cooked and served in an earthenware pot called a *pucara*. *Frango na pucara*, for example, is a

chicken casserole. In the south, particularly the Alentejo, the hinged, metal *cataplana*, which snaps shut like a clam and sizzles with anything the cook has decided to put in, is widely seen. Sometimes, meat and fish appear in the same dish, for example in dishes such as *cataplana alentejana*, which has both shellfish and pork in it. This is a particularly delicious combination.

WINES AND PORT

Port is Portugal's most famous liquid export. In Vila Nova de Gaia, opposite Porto, it is available for tasting free of charge in the many shippers' houses (➤ 55).

In general, Portuguese table wines emulate the food in being good, honest, full of character and unencumbered by too much subtlety or finesse. Internationally, the best known Portuguese wine is still *Mateus Rosé*, though others are now growing in prominence.

Among the light whites, dry, slightly sparkling *vinho verde* from the Minho is a

favourite all over the country and goes particularly well with fish and seafood. Other good whites to look for include wines from *Dão* and *Serradayres*. In the Algarve the very cheap local wines from *Lagoa* are good, but they don't travel well.

For reds, the big, gutsy wines from *Dão* and *Bairrada* in the Beiras are found all over the country and are good accompaniments to the wholesome country fare. A couple of more esoteric reds to look for include *Tinto da Anfora* and the excellent though expensive *Quinta da Bacaloa* made from French Cabernet Sauvignon grapes.

short break

If you only have a short time to visit Portugal and would like to take home some unforgettable memories, you can do something local and capture the real flavour of the country. The following suggestions will give you a wide range of sights and experiences that won't take long, won't cost very much and will make your visit very special.

● **Walk along the quayside in Lisbon's Belém district.** Admire the great 'Manueline' showpieces of the Jerónimos Monastery and the Belém Tower. You will not fail to sense the spirit of the great Portuguese explorers (➤ 44–45).

● **Sit in the shade of an Alentejo cork tree** or go for a walk through a forest of these beautiful trees whose thick bark is prized all over the world.

● **Eat a plate of sardines** grilled whole on charcoal. Have them plain, with just some lemon squeezed over them.

● **Ride on a tram** – in either Lisbon or Porto. Choose one of the clanking, turn-of-the-20th-century ones.

● **Go to a *fado* house.** The songs you will hear lay Portugal's soul bare, and express the notion of *saudade* – a deep longing for something lost (➤ 112, 142).

● **Stand on Europe's most southwesterly point,** Cabo de São Vicente. It is a suitably dramatic spot for the very corner of a continent. Ships on their way to or from the Mediterranean pass by incredibly close (➤ 40–41).

● **Visit Barcelos market** on Thursday morning, and barter with the best of them (► 91, 111).

● **Walk around the walls of Silves castle,** and feel the wraiths of the Moors, for whom this was once the capital of Al-Gharb – 'the Western Land' (► 178).

● **Drink a glass of port.**
Then another. What more needs to be said? Only that you must also try some chilled *vinho verde*.

● **Go to a village *festa*.**
These erupt all over the country, especially in summer, with religious processions, singing, dancing, eating and drinking as fireworks leave a whiff of gunpowder hanging in the air (➤ 24–25).

Planning

Before you go

WHEN TO GO

JAN	FEB	MAR	APR	MAY	JUN	JUL	AUG	SEP	OCT	NOV	DEC
12°C	12°C	13°C	16°C	17°C	21°C	22°C	23°C	21°C	18°C	15°C	12°C
54°F	54°F	55°F	61°F	63°F	70°F	72°F	73°F	70°F	64°F	59°F	54°F

High season   Low season

Spring and autumn are probably the best times to visit Portugal as the weather is mild and you avoid the huge crowds of mid-summer. In early spring you can catch the swathes of wild flowers covering the plains of the Alentejo and the delicate almond blossoms in the upper reaches of the Douro, while autum is great for catching the wine harvests. July and August are by far the busiest months as millions of tourists fly into Portugal (especially the Algarve) and Portuguese emigrants return to their villages to enjoy the constant summer *festas*. Be warned that summer temperatures in the interior can often exceed 40°C (104°F). If you are planning to visit the southern half of the country, winter can be an excellent option as these months tend to be mild by northern European standards, often with bright sunshine and clear skies.

WHAT YOU NEED

			UK	Germany	USA	Netherlands	Spain
●	Required	Some countries require a passport to remain valid for a minimum period (usually at least six months) beyond date of entry – contact their consulate or embassy or your travel agency for details					
○	Suggested						
▲	Not required						
Passport/National Identity Card (Valid for 6 months after entry)			●	●	●	●	●
Visa (regulations can change – check before booking your journey)			▲	▲	▲	▲	▲
Onward or Return Ticket			▲	▲	▲	▲	▲
Health Inoculations (tetanus)			▲	▲	▲	▲	▲
Health Documentation (reciprocal agreement; ➤ 23, Health Insurance)			○	○	▲	○	○
Travel Insurance			○	○	○	○	○
Driving Licence (national or International Driving Permit)			●	●	●	●	●
Car Insurance Certificate			●	●	●	●	●

WEBSITES

www.portugal.org
www.portugal.com
www.portugalonline.com
www.portugalinfo.net
www.portugalvirtual.pt

www.visitalgarve.pt
www.visitlisboa.com
www.portotourism.pt
www.the-news.net
www.travel.state.gov

TOURIST OFFICES AT HOME

In the UK

Portuguese National Tourist Office,
Portuguese Embassy
11 Belgrave Square,
London SW1X 8PP
☎ 0845 355 1212;
www.portugalinsite.com

In the USA

Portuguese Trade and Tourism
Office, 590 Fifth Avenue,
3rd Floor,
New York
NY 10036–4702
☎ 646/723-0200
www.visitportugal.com

HEALTH INSURANCE

EU nationals receive emergency medical treatment with the relevant documentation (EHIC – European Health Insurance Card), but medical insurance is still advised and is essential for all other visitors. US visitors should check their insurance coverage.

Dental treatment for EU nationals is very limited under the state scheme. You will probably have to pay and the charges are not refundable; other visitors will certainly have to pay. Check if private medical insurance will cover you.

TIME DIFFERENCES

GMT	Portugal	Germany	USA (NY)	Netherlands	Spain
12 noon	12 noon	1PM	7AM	1PM	1PM

Portuguese time is the same as Greenwich Mean Time. The clocks are advanced one hour in spring, and brought back one hour in autumn. Continental Europe is always one hour ahead.

NATIONAL HOLIDAYS

1 Jan *New Year's Day*
Feb/Mar *Shrove Tuesday*
Mar/Apr *Good Friday*
25 Apr *Liberty Day*
1 May *Labour Day*

May/Jun *Corpus Christi*
10 Jun *Portugal Day*
15 Aug *Feast of the Assumption*
5 Oct *Republic Day*

1 Nov *All Saints' Day*
1 Dec *Independence Day*
8 Dec *Feast of the Immaculate Conception*
25 Dec *Christmas Day*

WHAT'S ON WHEN

All Portuguese towns have their own *festas* (details from tourist offices), but these are Portugals's major festivals. Precise dates can vary.

February

Carnival weekend (which precedes Lent): festivities all over the country with streamers, firecrackers, water pistols and fancy dress. Particularly lively celebrations at Loulé in the Algarve, with processions through the streets and mock battles fought with almond blossoms.

March

Holy Week: processions and festivals take place all over Portugal during the week leading up to Easter. The greatest concentration of these is in the north. On Good Friday, crowds gather to do penance in Braga, religious capital of Portugal, in preparation for the Easter celebrations.

May

Festas das Cruzes (Feast of the Crosses) in Barcelos (first weekend): 16 crosses symbolizing the Passion of Christ are erected to mark a procession route carpeted with flowers.
Fátima Day (13 May): this is the anniversary of the first apparition of the Virgin Mary to three shepherd children at Fátima in 1917.

June

Festa de São Gonçalo (the Feast of Saint Gonçalo) in Amarante (first weekend of the month).
Festas dos Santos Populares (Feasts of the People's Saints) in Lisbon (12–29 Jun). June is the capital's month of merrymaking, with the greatest festivities on the feast of Santo António on 12 and 13 Jun.

Porto's greatest festival, *São João* (St John), coincides with the summer solstice. Bonfires are lit and a huge firework display is staged (last week in Jun).

June/July
International Film Festival – Portugal's longest running film festival showcasing short films from around the world. Mainly shown in Portrimão.

July/August
Festas da Rainha Santa (Festivals of the Holy Queen) in Coimbra. A week

of cultural events (first week of Jul).
The National Handicrafts Fair in Vila do Conde, on the Minho coast (last week of Jul/first week of Aug).
Festas da Senhora da Agonia (Feast of Our Lady of Suffering). Otherwise known as the *Festas de Viana*, this is one of the greatest and most popular festivals in Portugal (Fri–Sun nearest 29 Aug).

September
The wine harvest festival at Palmela, across the Tagus from Lisbon (second Sun in Sep).

November
National Gastronomic Fair in Santarém in the Ribatejo with samples of food and wine from all the different regions of Portugal (first week in Nov).

Getting there

BY AIR

Lisbon (Portela de Sacavem) Airport

7km (4 miles) to city centre

N/A

30 minutes

15 minutes

Faro Airport

4km (2.5 miles) to city centre

N/A

15 minutes

10 minutes

Portugal has three international airports – Lisbon, Porto and Faro. Scheduled and charter flights arrive daily at all of them from the UK and the rest of Europe, and there are direct flights to Lisbon, and charter flights to Porto, from North America.

BY BUS

International bus services to various destinations in Portugal are available from the UK via Paris, operated by Eurolines (www.eurolines.com). Transfer times in Paris can sometimes be quite long, so it may be worth making your own way to Paris to avoid the wait.

BY TRAIN

You can travel from Waterloo, London to Lisbon, Portugal via Paris and Madrid, although the cost can be high when compared to budget flight deals and the journey time long (25–30 hours). For more information check Eurostar at www.eurostar.com and Rail Europe at www.raileurope.co.uk.

BY CAR

It's a long drive to Portugal from the UK but it can be worth it if part of an extended holiday through France and Spain. Ferrying your car to northern Spain can cut down on driving time, though it is still a long journey from the northern Spanish ports of Santander or Bilbao down to Portugal (Santander–Lisbon 833km/518 miles; Bilbao–Lisbon 865km/538 miles).

Getting around

PUBLIC TRANSPORT

Internal flights TAP Air Portugal ☎ 707 205 700; www.flytap.pt and Portugália ☎ 707 789 090; www.pga.pt connect Lisbon, Porto and Faro. Portugália operates a Ponte Areo (Air Bridge) commuter service between Lisbon and Porto/Faro; no advance booking is needed, just turn up. Charter flights are also available.

Trains The national railway company, Caminhos de Ferro Portugueses (CP) ☎ 808 208 208; www.cp.pt, runs three types of service: Regional (stopping at most stations); Intercidade (stopping at only a few large towns); and Rápido (express train between Lisbon and Porto). Fares are reasonable with many discount schemes.

Long-distance buses There is a wide variety of private bus companies which cover most of the country, much more extensively than the rail network. Long distance buses are mostly comfortable.

Ferries Ferries from Lisbon cross the Rio Tejo to the suburb of Cacilhas every 10 to 15 minutes (from 7am to 9pm) from Terminal Fluvial, adjacent to Praça do Comércio, or from Cais de Sodré every 15 minutes (24-hour service). From Setúbal there is a 24-hour service across to the Tróia Peninsula, at least hourly, with a journey time of 20 minutes.

Urban transport In the main towns there is a complete public transport network. In Lisbon the state-owned Carris company runs buses, the underground (Metropolitano), quaint electric trams *(eléctricos)*, and funiculars and lifts (both called *elevadores*). Useful guide: *Rede de Transportes Públicos*.

TAXIS

Taxis are cream in colour. In towns meters should be used; make sure that they are switched on. Tips are discretionary. Outside urban areas the charge is per kilometre. Between 10pm and 6am the rate increases by 20 per cent.

DRIVING

- The Portuguese drive on the right side of the road.

- Seat belts must be worn in front seats at all times and in rear seats where fitted.

- Random breath testing takes place. Never drive under the influence of alcohol.

- Fuel *(gasolina)* is available in three grades: *super* (98 octane), *sem chumbo* (unleaded 95 octane), and *super sem chumbo* (unleaded 98 octane). Prices vary by a few cents around the country. Filling stations are open 8am to midnight (some 24 hours). The carrying of fuel in cans in cars is forbidden.

- Speed limits are as follows:
  Speed limit on motorways (autoestradas): 120kph (74mph); minimum: 40kph (25mph)
  Speed limit on dual carriageways: 100kph (62mph); country roads: 90kph (56mph)
  Speed limits on urban roads: 50kph (31mph)

- Orange SOS telephones are located at regular intervals along motorways and other main roads. A breakdown service is operated by the national motoring organization, the Automóvel Club de Portugal (ACP). For assistance from the club, ☎ 707 509 510; www.acp.pt. Place a red warning triangle 30m (33yds) behind your vehicle and put on your fluorescent yellow safety vest.

CAR RENTAL

Prices are relatively cheap. You will find the major international companies in Lisbon, Porto and the Algarve. If using one of the many local firms offering competitive rates, check the vehicle is in good condition and that adequate insurance is included.

FARES AND CONCESSIONS

Students/youths The International Student Identity Card (ISIC) for students, and the International Youth Card (IYC) for those under 26, entitles holders to discounts on transport and fees for museums and attractions. The Cartão Jovem (youth card), for those between 12 and 26, gives a 50 per cent discount on rail journeys over 50km (30 miles).

Senior citizens Winter holidays in the Algarve are popular with older travellers. Low-cost, flight-only deals are available from some countries, and you can find long-term accommodation for a fraction of the high-season rate. Over 65s (with proof of age) receive a 50 per cent reduction on all trains.

Being there

TOURIST OFFICES

Visitors can call free phone 808 781 212 for information from across Portugal.

Costa de Lisboa
Turismo de Lisboa,
Rua do Arsenal 15,
1100–038 Lisboa (Lisbon)
☎ 210 312 700

Costa de Prata
Região de Turismo do Centro, Largo da Portagem, 3000–337 Coimbra
☎ 239 488 120

Costa Verde
Comissão Municipal de Turismo do Porto, Rua Clube dos Fenianos 25, 4000–172 Oporto (Porto)
☎ 223 393 470

Montanhas
Região de Turismo de Dão Lafões,
Avenida Gulbenkian,
3510–055 Viseu
☎ 232 420 950

Planícies
Região de Turismo de Évora,
Rua de Aviz 90,
7000–591 Évora
☎ 266 730 440

Algarve
Região de Turismo do Algarve,
Avenida 5 de Outubro 18,
8000–076 Faro
☎ 289 800 400

MONEY

The Portuguese unit of currency is the euro (€). Notes are in denominations of €5, €10, €20, €50, €100 and €200, and coins are in denominations of 1, 2, 5, 10 and 20 cents, and €1 and €2. Euro travellers' cheques are accepted, as are major credit cards in large towns and cities. Credit and debit cards can be used for withdrawing euros from cashpoints.

TIPS/GRATUITIES

Yes ✓	No ✗		
Restaurants (if service not included)		✓	10%
Cafés/bars		✓	10%
Taxis		✓	10%
Tour guides (discretionary)		✓	€1
Porters		✓	€1
Chambermaids		✗	
Hairdressers		✓	10%
Toilets (rest rooms)		✗	

POSTAL SERVICES

There is at least one *correio* (post office) in every town and reasonably large village. They sell *selos* (stamps) as do many places with a *correio* sign. In small towns they close for lunch, otherwise hours are: Mon–Fri 8:30–6. Letters to European countries usually arrive within five to seven days, to the USA within ten days. Send urgent post by correio azul and put it in a blue postbox. Other postboxes are red.

TELEPHONES

Most public telephones now accept coins and credit cards or phone cards. Phone cards can be bought at newsagents and in bars and can be used for international calls. Most hotels will also have international direct dialling but will add a large premium to the bill. Check the hotel's pricing policy before making a call.

International Dialling Codes

From Portugal to:
UK: 00 44
Germany: 00 49
USA: 00 1
Netherlands: 00 31
Spain: 00 34

Emergency Telephone Numbers

Police: 112
Ambulance: 112
Fire: 112
Forest safety: 117

EMBASSIES AND CONSULATES

UK: ☎ 213 924 000
Germany: ☎ 218 810 210
USA: ☎ 217 273 300

Netherlands: ☎ 213 914 900
Spain: ☎ 213 472 381

HEALTH ADVICE

Sun advice Sunburn and sunstroke are common problems in summer (especially during July and August), particularly in the south of the country. Do not be deceived by a cooling wind off the Atlantic. Avoid prolonged exposure and use a sunscreen or cover up.

Drugs Prescription and non-prescription drugs and medicines are available from pharmacies *(farmácias)*, distinguished by a large green cross. Pharmacists have a high degree of training and can prescribe remedies for a wide range of ailments.

Safe water Tap water is generally safe but not too pleasant. Anywhere, but especially outside the main cities, towns and resorts, it is advisable to drink bottled water (água mineral), either *sem gás* (still) or *com gás* (carbonated).

PERSONAL SAFETY

Violence against tourists is unusual in Portugal. Theft from cars and other petty crime is increasingly a problem, especially in the Algarve. Car stereos are particularly at risk. The Polícia de Segurança Pública are the urban police to whom any crime should be reported; in tourist areas, some wear red armbands with CD on them. Remember:

● Never leave anything of value in your car.
● Do not leave valuables on the beach or poolside.
● Leave valuables in hotel safe deposit boxes.
● Don't walk alone through dimly lit areas at night.

Police assistance: ☎ 112 from any call box

ELECTRICITY

The local power supply is: 220 volts. Sockets take two-round-pin continental-style plugs. Visitors from the UK require an adaptor and US visitors a voltage transformer.

OPENING HOURS

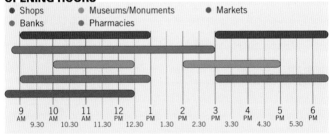

In addition to the times in the chart above, most shops close at 1pm on Saturday and are closed Sundays. In shopping centres located in cities and larger towns shops are open 10am up to 11pm daily. In tourist resorts and cities some supermarkets are open until 9pm. Hypermarkets are open 10am to 11pm. As for pharmacies, each area has a pharmacy open until midnight, the location of which is advertised on pharmacy doors.

Most museums stick roughly to the opening times in the chart, but many close Monday, while some places also close Wednesday.

LANGUAGE

A knowledge of Spanish and/or French makes Portuguese easy to read, but speaking it is somewhat trickier. Portuguese sounds very different from Spanish. Even so, most Portuguese understand Spanish and in tourist areas English is widely spoken. Knowing a few Portuguese words will make your trip more rewarding. Below is a list of some words that might be useful. The AA's *Essential Portuguese Phrase Book* lists over 2,000 phrases and 2,000 words.

hotel	*hotel*	rate	*preço*
room single/	*quarto simples/*	breakfast	*pequeno almoço*
double	*de casal*	toilet	*sanita*
one/two nights	*um/duas noite(s)*	bath/shower	*banheira/duche*
reservation	*reserva*	balcony	*varanda*
bank	*banco*	pound sterling	*libra esterlina*
exchange office	*casa de câmbio*	American dollar	*dólar americano*
post office	*correio*	exchange rate	*câmbio*
money	*dinheiro*	bank card	*cartão do banco*
foreign currency	*moeda estrangeira*	credit card	*cartão de crédito*
restaurant	*restaurante*	daily fixed menu	*ementa turística*
bar/café	*café*	wine list	*lista de vinhos*
table	*mesa*	lunch	*almoço*
menu	*ementa*	dinner	*jantar*
aeroplane/airport	*avião/aeroporto*	single/return	*ida/ida e volta*
flight	*vôo*	first/second class	*primeira/segunda*
train/train station	*comboio/estação*		*classe*
	de comboios	bus/bus station	*autocarro/estação de*
ticket	*bilhete*		*camionetas*
yes/no	*sim/não*	help!	*ajuda!*
please	*se faz favor*	today/tomorrow	*hoje/amanhã*
thank you	*obrigado*	yesterday	*ontem*
hello/goodbye	*óla/adeus*	how much?	*quanto?*
excuse me!	*desculpe!*	open/closed	*aberto/fechado*

Best places to see

1 Alcobaça

One of the most beautiful and atmospheric buildings in Portugal and a shrine to a poignant love story.

The Real Abadia de Santa Maria de Alcobaça (the Royal Abbey of St Mary) was built on the orders of King Afonso I to fulfil a promise he had made to God before a victory over the Moors at Santarém. It was given to the Cistercian order and became immensely rich and

powerful, in the finest traditions of medieval monasticism. The monks remained at Alcobaça until the Abbey's confiscation during repression of religious orders in the 19th century. Today, the monastery still dominates this small agricultural town surrounded by fruit-growing estates and vineyards.

The church, the largest in Portugal, is gloriously spacious and built in a refreshingly simple style, as are the 14th-century cloisters where a calming aura lingers, especially if you are able to wander round in silence. More worldly are the gigantic kitchens and monastic cooking utensils.

But it is the tombs of Dom Pedro and Inês de Castro which attract the greatest attention. The pair are Portuguese history's irrepressible lovers – Pedro was a prince and Inês the daughter of a nobleman from Galicia. Pedro's father, King Afonso, had her murdered to avoid allowing the Galicians influence in Portuguese affairs. Pedro rebelled against his father and two years later became king, holding the memory of Inês dear for the rest of his life. Both were buried at Alcobaça in tombs with intricate carvings telling their story; the tombs are toe-to-toe so that the first thing they see on Judgement Day will be each other.

➕ 1K 🖂 20km (12.5 miles) south of Batalha 🕙 Apr–Sep daily 9–7; Oct–Mar 9–5 ✋ Church free; monastery moderate (Sun 9–2 free) 🚌 Buses from Lisbon (2 hours) and Leiria (45 mins)
ℹ Praça 25 de Abril, opposite abbey ☎ 262 582 377

2 Batalha

Batalha is one of the architectural jewels of Portugal and a symbol of independence from Spain.

Batalha means 'battle', referring to a promise by King João I that if he defeated the Castilian army, he would build a great monastery and dedicate it to the Virgin. The victory took place in 1385 at nearby Aljubarrota; although greatly outnumbered, João's

military commander, Constable Nun' Alvares Pereira, put the Castilians to flight. The massive building project began in 1388, eventually becoming a Dominican abbey.

The towering honey-coloured church with its spires, pinnacles, flying buttresses and gargoyles comes startlingly into view as you round a corner on the N1. The sheer dimensions are awesome – the nave is 80m (262ft) long by 32m high (105ft). King João and his Queen, Philippa of Lancaster, lie entombed in the octagonal Capela do

Fundador (Founders' Chapel), their stone-carved effigies resting, hand in hand, under a stone canopy emblazoned with the coats of arms of Lancaster and the House of Avis. Nearby lie the tombs of their six sons, including Prince Henry the Navigator.

Among the other finest features are the Capelas Imperfeitas (unfinished chapels), decorated with carvings of Manueline (named after Manuel I, under whom the style flourished) flamboyance; the Royal Cloisters, with intricately carved Manueline embellishments to the original Gothic; and the beautifully vaulted Chapterhouse, containing the tombs of unknown soldiers killed in World War I and in the African wars.

✠ 1K ✉ 11km (7 miles) south of Leiria ⏱ Apr–Sep daily 9–6; Oct–Mar 9–5 ✋ Church free; monastery moderate 🚌 Bus stop on Largo da Misericórdia
🅸 Praça Mouzinho de Albuquerque ☎ 244 765 180

Cabo de São Vicente

A raw, wild, windswept headland at the very corner of Europe, punctuated with a huge lighthouse.

Cabo de São Vincente, 6km (4 miles) along the cliff top road from Sagres, is the most southwesterly promontory of Europe. Here the rock face is sheer and grey, dropping several hundred metres into the sea. Ships, on their way to the Mediterranean, pass by unbelievably close. Further out, sharks are caught from small fishing boats. Land-based anglers perch precariously on the cliff edges, casting their long lines way down into the deep Atlantic. Tales are told of the less wary, hooking a sizeable fish and being yanked to their deaths, over the cliff.

The only building is a lighthouse, which you can climb if it happens to be open – there are no published times – to see the 3,000-watt bulb which projects its beam 90km (56 miles) out to sea. Outside, stalls sell thick woollen shirts and socks; tourists, who often arrive wearing T-shirts and shorts, make easy prey as they are caught offguard by the chill wind which blows even in summer.

For some, the cape appears a god-forsaken place – out on a bare, windswept plain dotted with scrub and the occasional stunted, crouching fig tree. The few nearby Moorish-style villages of whitewashed walls and red tiles are tightly huddled, as if sheltering from the wind. Others appreciate the raw, solitary beauty of this landscape.

In March, April, September and October, huge flocks of migrating birds use the cape as a staging post on their journeys between Europe and Africa.

✚ 8Y ✉ 6km (4 miles) west of Sagres ⏰ Access to the cape at any time. No official timetable for the opening of the lighthouse 👋 Free 🚌 Buses from Sagres

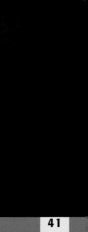

4 Monsaraz

**One of Portugal's most spectacular
fortified hilltop villages, nestling
within impregnable stone walls.**

Monsaraz is one of a long chain of fortified
villages near Portugal's eastern border with
Spain, built for their commanding positions;
Romans, Visigoths and Moors all had
settlements here, before the Christian re-
conquest. The village itself has a sleepy,
medieval mien – the main street is too
narrow for a car; park outside the main gate.

The present castle and formidable
ramparts are 14th-century, built by King
Dinis. In front of the pentagonal castle
keep is a square where bullfights are held
on feast days with villagers cheering from
the walls.

The view from the parapet is stunning:
the plains of the Alentejo stretch out
endlessly towards the coast, whose outline
just becomes visible on the horizon when

the air is exceptionally clear. The rocky, meandering Guadiana river to the east provides a dramatic contrast, while Spain extends beyond like a crumpled rug.

There are several points of interest on Rua Direita, the cobbled main street, which is lined with houses emblazoned with the coats of arms of wealthy 16th- to 17th-century families. The Paços do Concelho Tribunal building has a 15th-century fresco depicting a judge being tempted by an impish, bride-offering devil while simultaneously being drawn into the outstretched arms and majestic justice of Christ.

The Igreja Matriz parish church is also worth a look.

✚ 12U ✉ Southeast of Évora, 7km (4 miles) off N256
🍴 Restaurants and cafés, including Solar de Monsaraz (€€) 🚌 Daily bus service from Évora (45 mins)
🛈 Largo Dom Nuno Alvares Pereira ☎ 266 557 136

5 Mosteiro dos Jerónimos

www.mosteirojeronimos.pt

The crowning glory of Manueline architecture, built on riches which followed the discovery of trade routes to the east.

Jerónimos is the classic example of Manueline architecture. The monastery is built on the site of the Santa Maria hermitage, which Prince Henry the Navigator founded in 1460, the year of his death. This was hugely embellished by Dom Manuel in the following century to commemorate Vasco da

Gama's discovery of the sea route to India in 1498.

Accordingly, the buildings are adorned with ocean-going and oriental motifs such as seahorses, elephants, ropes and armillary spheres, all elaborately carved in stone. The southern façade, looking out over the Tagus estuary, is sensationally grand. A bearded statue of Prince Henry stands at the south portal. Dom Manuel and his wife Dona Maria preside over the west portal, in the company of the four original evangelists.

Most breathtaking of all is the cavernous interior; six great supporting columns are styled as colossal palm trees with fanned ribbed vaulting as their fronds. Inside are the tombs and stone effigies of several kings supported by elephants, and of two of Portugal's greatest heroes – Vasco da Gama himself, and Luis de Camões, who told the story of his discoveries in the epic poem *Os Lusíadas*.

The monastery was seriously damaged in the 1755 earthquake but many splendid features survived unscathed, including the majestic west portal. The cloisters are on two floors, carved with fantastic and surreal animals and distorted human figures secreted among intricate vegetation.

✚ *Lisboa 1d (off map)* ✉ Belém, Lisbon ⏰ May–Sep Tue–Sun 10–6; Oct–Apr Tue–Sun 10–5 💷 Church free; cloisters moderate (free Sun until 2pm) 🚌 Buses from the Baixa district; tram 15 🚉 On Avenida de Brasília Belém Station on Cascais line ⛴ Ferry to Trafaria, across Tagus

6 Museu Calouste Gulbenkian

www.gulbenkian.pt

An astounding collection of artistic riches from across the centuries, bequeathed by the oil magnate.

Calouste Gulbenkian was an Armenian oil magnate who, shortly after the turn of the 20th century, acquired a five per cent share in the oil fields of

Iraq. As the 20th century progressed, the world's dependence on the internal combustion engine burgeoned and Gulbenkian grew phenomenally wealthy. In 1942 he adopted Portugal, neutral during World War II, as his homeland.

He died in Lisbon in 1955, bequeathing his vast array of treasures and huge fortune to the establishment of a foundation for 'charitable, artistic, educational and scientific' purposes. The foundation's assets now make it the largest charity in Europe.

The museum, set in beautiful green gardens, was opened by the foundation in 1969, and includes seven principal collections: Egyptian art; Greco-Roman art; Middle Eastern and Islamic art; Oriental art; a collection of French ivories; painting and sculpture (including works by Rembrandt, Rubens, Gainsborough and Manet, and a superb marble statue of Diana by Houbon), and furniture and furnishings.

The museum also houses smaller, rare collections, such as snuff boxes, French bookbindings, European ceramics, art nouveau jewellery and gold and silver work.

Across the gardens from the main museum is the Centro de Arte Moderna (Modern Art Centre), a new extension opened in 1983. The centre houses both permanent and temporary exhibitions, with a strong emphasis on 20th-century Portuguese artists such as Almada Negreiros, who was the founder of the school of Portuguese Modernism. There is also some excellent modern sculpture on display in the centre, including work by Henry Moore.

✚ *Lisboa 2a (off map)* ✉ Avenida da Berna 45, Lisbon
🕐 Tue–Sun 10–6. Modern Art Museum Tue–Sun 10–5:45. Closed public hols 🎫 Tue–Sat inexpensive, Sun free
🍴 Café-bar (€€) Ⓜ São Sebastião or Praça de Espanha
🚌 746

7 Óbidos

An enchanting hilltop town, beloved of artists and poets and traditionally given as a wedding gift by Portuguese kings to their queens.

Óbidos is enclosed within massive, crenellated 13th-century walls punctuated with huge, round towers out of all proportion to the Lilliputian buildings within. Not a single modern structure is to be found; instead, there are scaled-down versions of typically Portuguese baroque churches, cottages, worn stone staircases and alleyways.

There are about 5,000 inhabitants, including many poets and artists drawn by the romanticism of Óbidos, and villagers whose families have lived here for generations, and who still have their diminutive vegetable patches at the base of the great walls.

At the highest point, set against the walls, is the castle, which became a royal palace in the 16th century. It has been converted into an atmospheric *pousada* (state-run hotel).

A leisurely walk around the entire walls, which includes some fairly steep climbing, takes about an hour. A good place to start is at the main gate at the bottom of the town, but there are several other staircases up the 14m-high (46ft) ramparts to tremendous vantage points Looking beyond the walls, there are wonderful vistas over the Laguna de Óbidos (Óbidos Lagoon) – the inlet is now silted up but it once made Óbidos a sea port.

To look out west from the walls, towards the coast and horizon beyond as a blood-red sunset dims into twilight, can be an achingly romantic experience.

➕ 8R ✉ 22km (13.5 miles) inland from Peniche
🚌 Bus stop by the Porta da Vila 🚋 Train station outside the walls. Lisbon 2 hours
ℹ Rua Direita, in car park at entrance to town
☎ 262 955 060

8 Serra da Estrela

www.rt-serradaestrela.pt

This range of soaring mountains, interspersed with glacial valleys, is a real treat for hikers and nature-lovers.

Between Coimbra and the Spanish border is Portugal's highest mountain range and national park – the rugged Serra da Estrela, whose crowning peak, the Torre, reaches almost 2,000m (6,560ft). Yet despite having some of the most spectacular scenery in the country, this sparsely populated region is still relatively unknown to outsiders.

When snow falls, a few optimistic skiers make for the two very limited runs which constitute the sum total of Portuguese winter sports; in spring the occasional lonesome nature-lover can be found on the wild, flower-blanketed mountainsides; in autumn you might come across a hunter dangling a hare or partridge from his belt; in summer the streams dry up and the verdant valleys turn brown and inhospitable.

Nevertheless, a diversion through the Serra da Estrela is highly recommended for those driving between Lisbon or the Alentejo and the north with time to spare. Particularly sensational are the N232 between Manteigas and Gouveia, and the Vale Glaciario do Zêzere (Zêzere Glacial Valley) which connects the N232 just south of Manteigas, with the N239 to Covilhã. The latter junction is a short distance from the Torre. There is a wonderfully located modern *pousada* near Manteigas, which is an excellent base for touring or walking.

Look for the rich, creamy Serra da Estrela cheese made from ewes' milk and sold by the roadside in pats wrapped in paper. The runny version is the tastiest, oozing out of cracks in its rind.

🔀 4G 🍴 Restaurants of all categories in the region 🚌 All the main towns of the area are connected by bus, though services are often scant 🚉 Covilhã has a train station, 4km (2.5 miles) out of town
ℹ️ Serra da Estrela regional office, Avenida Frei Heitor Pinto, Covilhã ☎ 275 319 560

9 Tavira

A delightful, historic little town in the far east of the Algarve which is touched rather than engulfed by tourism.

One of the Algarve's most beautiful towns lies beyond the marshes, salt pans, lagoons and flat sandy islands east of Faro. A string of elegant, 18th-century classical façades lines the waterfront along the River Gilão, spanned by two bridges, one of them originally Roman though most of the existing structure is 17th century. There are also gardens fronting the river, adjacent to the arcaded central Praça da República, and a covered market.

Tavira's prosperity was built on tuna fishing, mainly during the 16th to 18th centuries. Vast shoals used to migrate past this shoreline every summer, falling prey to the harpoons of the Tavira fleet. The giant, thrashing fish were hauled in and put to death by the fishermen amid bloody rituals which became known as the 'bullfights of the sea'.

This wealth accounts for the town's 21 churches; finest is Igreja do Carmo, where, beyond a simple façade, you are greeted by an unexpected riot of

baroque. None of the churches has official opening times – just try your luck. There is also a ruined castle reached by a cobbled alley from the Praça da República. From here, there are some commanding views over the town.

Offshore is the Ilha de Tavira (Tavira Island), an 11km-long (7-mile) bar of sand which, despite the lack of shade, is one of the Algarve's best beaches east of Faro. Regular ferries leave from a jetty at Quatro Aguas, 2km (1.2 miles) from the town centre, and take just a few minutes.

🏛 11Y ✉ 30km (18 miles) east of Faro 🍴 Many restaurants (€–€€€) 🚌 Bus station on the Rua dos Pelames, near the Praça da República 🚆 Train station at end of Rua da Liberdade, 1km (0.5 miles) from town centre 🛈 Rua da Galeria 9 ☎ 281 322511

10 Vila Nova de Gaia

Discover the long and rich history of Portugal's most famous 'liquid asset', then sample the product.

Across the double-decker Dom Luis I bridge, opposite Porto, is Vila Nova de Gaia, home of port wine. Whitewashed onto red-tiled roofs, lit up at night in giant neon signs, and adorning the sails of traditional *barco rabelo* boats on the waterfront, are the familiar names of the great British port-shipping houses – Taylor, Graham, Cockburn, Sandeman – along with Portuguese houses such as Cálem and Ferreira.

Many of the port houses offer free guided tours of the so-called 'lodges' – a corruption of the Portuguese word *loja*, meaning 'warehouse'. You can wander through the ancient, cobwebbed corridors walled with barrels of port ageing in oak and learn how, in the 17th and 18th centuries, hostilities with France led British merchants to venture into the harsh, mountainous terrain of the upper Douro valley in search of alternative sources of wine.

The brandy they added to preserve the wine during the hot journey downriver to Vila Nova de Gaia led to the birth of the fortifying process. Let your taste buds explore the many different styles of port: the aperitif, dry white port; light, amber-coloured tawny, made from wines up to a century old blended with fresh young wine; rich, full-bodied ruby port; and finally, vintage port, declared only in exceptionally good years, bottled after two years, matured in black bottles, and the flagship of every shipper's range.

Take care not to stagger into the Douro when the tour has finished and you re-cross the river to Porto.

✚ 2E 🕐 Similar tours and tastings are conducted at the various lodges. Opening times are generally Mon–Fri 9:30/10–12 and 2:15–5:30. In summer, many also open on Sat 🍽 Restaurants of all categories in Gaia 🚌 57 from Praça Almeida Garret (near São Bento train station) ℹ Avenida Diogo Leite 242 ☎ 223 703 735

Best things to do

Good places to have lunch

Adega Regional Kilowatt (€)
Artisan-produced air-dried ham in country bread accompanied by *vinho verde* at this tiny rustic eatery.
✉ Rua 31 de Janeiro, Amarante ☎ 255 433 159

Adega Vila Lisa (€€)
To sample Algarve cuisine at its best sit back and enjoy Adega Vila Lisa's fixed four-course menu.
✉ Rua Francisco Bívar 52, Portimão ☎ 282 968 478

Café Inglês (€)
Elegant 1920s mansion, now a café, serving a good range of Portuguese and international snacks.
✉ Escadas do Castelo II, Silves ☎ 282 442 585

Dona Barca (€)
Behind the fishing quay, this simple place offers great value for money and the freshest fish cooked on its patio grill.
✉ Largo da Barca 9, Portimão ☎ 282 484 189

Jardim dos Frangos (€)
Grilled chicken and sardines with fresh salad form the main menu items at this exceptional budget restaurant. Busy.
✉ Avenida dos Combatentes da Grande Guerra 168, Cascais
☎ 214 861 717

Nicola (€)
A grand, old-fashioned café in Lisbon's Baixa district. Perfect for a snack as you watch the world go by.
✉ Praça Dom Pedro IV 24–25, Lisbon ☎ 213 460 579

Paraíso da Montanha (€€)
Sensational views and excellent spicy chicken *piri-piri*.
✉ On the road from Monchique up to Foia ☎ 282 912 150

Pousada de São Filipe (€€€)

The magnificent views from the terrace atop the fortress walls match the food served at this most dramatic *pousada*.

✉ Fortress São Filipe, Setúbal ☎ 265 550 070

Pousada de São Francisco (€€)

Feast on superbly prepared Alentejo specialities in the old monastic refectory.

✉ Beja ☎ 284 313 580

Solar de Monsaraz (€€)

The best place in town to sample some hearty Alentejo dishes.

✉ Rua Conde de Monsaraz 38, Monsaraz ☎ 266 502 846

Top activities

Big-game fishing: The Algarve is one of the few places in Europe where you can fish shark and tuna. Centres at Portimão (☎ 282 415 136 and Vilamoura (☎ 289 315 234).

Birdwatching: Trips are organized by Quinta do Barranco da Estrada in the Alentejo (☎ 283 933 065).

Golf: Portugal is one of Europe's top golfing destinations. Top courses include Penina (☎ 282 420 200) and Quinta do Lago (☎ 289 390 705) in the Algarve.

Horse-back riding: There are many riding centres in the Algarve, including one at Vilamoura (☎ 289 302 577) and one at Quinta dos Amigos near Almansil (☎ 289 395 269).

Sailing: Good facilities for boat rental at Vilamoura. Also, yacht clubs at Lagos, Ferragudo and Carvoeiro.

Surfing: Best places are Ericeira, the west coast of the Algarve and Guincho on the Lisbon coast.

Swimming: The Algarve has some of Europe's finest beaches, such as the beautiful Praia Dona Ana and Praia do Camilo. On the Arrábida coast, Sesimbra's beach is one of the best.

Tennis: Portugal's top tennis schools are the David Lloyd Centre at Vilamoura, and the Jonathan Markson Centre at Praia da Luz.

Walking: Best regions for hikers are the Peneda-Gerês National Park in the far north, and the central Serra da Estrela.

Water parks: There are several in the Algarve, including Aqualand near Silves (➤ 69), and Slide and Splash at Estombar, near Lagoa (➤ 68).

a drive around the Douro Valley

From the lower level of the Dom Luis bridge, meander up the north bank of the river, passing two dams, before arriving at Peso da Régua.

Régua (as it is signposted, and always known) is one of the main port-producing cities, although it offers little to see or do. Better to continue on through the increasingly wild and spectacular scenery.

Cross the road bridge to the south bank of the Douro. From here, a beautiful route follows the river, which is turned into a long, serpentine lake by a huge hydro-electric dam. An iron bridge crosses the river at Pinhão.

Pinhão is a small town at the heart of the port-producing country. The red-tiled roofs of long, barrel warehouses are, as in Vila Nova de Gaia, whitewashed with the familiar names of the great port-shipping companies. The town itself, however, has little to detain the visitor, other than some beautiful azulejo tiles on the station platform, depicting traditional Douro rural life.

Another spectacular road twists up the valley of the Pinhão tributary, through dramatic, rocky scenery with mountainsides carved into terraces of vineyards, olive groves and citrus orchards which have been hewn and blasted out of the rock. This road leads up to the small

town of Alijó. From here, take the road to Pópulo, to join the main IP4 Porto/Braganza highway. Pull off the IP4 at the Vila Real signpost, and follow signposts to Sabrosa and Solar de Mateus, which is 3km (2 miles) south of the town.

Solar De Mateus is a splendid, 18th-century palace famous the world over for gracing the label of every bottle of Mateus Rosé sold. There is no other particular connection between between the palace and the wine, so don't expect a tasting. A tour of the treasure-filled palace and beautiful grounds, however, is a treat.

Turn off the IP4 at the Amarante signpost, to explore this lovely town (▶ 89). Re-join the IP4 (now a motorway) to return to central Porto. There is a toll to pay before you reach the city.

Distance About 330km (205 miles)
Time 10 hours, including stops
Start point Low Level, Dom Luis I Bridge, Porto ✚ *Porto 4c*
End point Porto city centre ✚ *Porto 3b*
Lunch Pousada Barão de Forrester (€€€€) ✉ Alijó ☎ 259 959 467

Top souvenir ideas

Azulejos Available as mass-produced tiles at tourist spots or as tasteful panels replicating designs of the 17th and 18th centuries.

Ceramics and pottery From rustic terracotta ovenware and ubiquitous Barcelos cockerels to hand-painted figurines and fine porcelain from Aveiro's renowned Vista Alegre factory.

Food Choose from cheeses (some can be expensive), olive oils, non-perishable Elvas plums, Madeira honey cake and dried fruits.

Glass Colourful, modern designs are available at good prices in Marinha Grande, as is fine crystal from Atlantis in Alcobaça.

Jewellery The north is considered the best place to buy jewellery, as it is home to the best craftsmen. Modern designs are available, but the region is best known for its gold filigree work.

Leather goods Great leather shoes are available at many of the regional markets, especially in the north. Also leather belts, bags, wallets and gloves.

Textiles Weavings, fines linens, embroideries, handmade cotton lace and the famous carpets from Arraiolos in the Alentejo.

Wine and other drinks Wherever you are in the country, you are never far from a demarcated wine zone, most of which still offer excellent value for money. Pick up a vintage port in Porto or some full-bodied reds from the Douro, Ribatejo or Alentejo. Don't forget *medronho*, the local liqueur from the Algarve, made from the arbutus berry.

Wooden crafts The distinctive Monchique folding stools are fairly easy to transport and make an unusual gift, as do the hand-painted trays and furniture (not so easily transported) from the Alentejo.

Best beaches

- Bordeira, Algarve west coast (➤ 77)

- Caminha, on the River Minho Estuary, bordering Spain

- Cascais, on the Lisbon coast (➤ 126)

- Ilha de Tavira, Algarve (➤ 52–53)

- Ofir, at the mouth of the Cávado, Minho

- Portinho da Arrábida, on the Arrábida coast (➤ 129)

- Praia do Camilo, near Lagos, Algarve

- Praia Tres Irmãos, near Portimão, Algarve

- São Martinho do Porto, near Leiria

- Vila Nova de Milfontes, Alentejo

Places to take the children

ALBUFEIRA
Krazy World-Algarve Zoo
A real mixture of things to do from swimming pools to petting zoo to exotic animal shows to a fairground.

✉ Signposted from N125, Algoz ☎ 282 574 134; www.krazyworld.com

Zoomarine
This aqua park features various different marine shows, including the ever-popular performing dolphins.

✉ N125 Guia ☎ 289 560 300; www.zoomarine.com

ALCOUTIM
Parque Mineiro Cova dos Mouros
This open-air museum re-creates the lifestyle of the Chalcolithic people who mined the site for gold and copper 5,000 years ago.

✉ 10km (6 miles) south of Martimlongo ☎ 281 489 505; http://minacovamouros.sitepac.pt

ALMANCIL
Carting Almancil
Karting track inaugurated by the late Ayrton Senna; a miniature version of the Brazilian F1 track.

✉ Sitio das Pereiras ☎ 289 399 899; www.mundokarting.pt

LAGOA
Slide and Splash
A huge complex of water chutes, slides and swimming pools to keep even the most reluctant of water-babies amused.

✉ N125, Vale de Deus, Estombar ☎ 282 340 800; www.slidesplash.com

LAGOS
Lagos Zoological Park
The land here has been transformed into various habitats for monkeys, wallabies and a range of exotic birds. There is also a

petting area with goats, ducks and chickens.

✉ Barão São João, north of Lagos

☎ 282 680 100; www.zoolagos.com

MONCHIQUE
Omega Parque Jardim Zoológico

Dedicated to the conservation and breeding of endangered species.

✉ On N266, Caldas de Monchique ☎ 282 911 327; www.omegaparque.com

PORTIMÃO
Pirate Ship Adventure Cruise

Enjoy cave exploration, sailing or beach BBQ from this fully rigged caravel sailing ship.

✉ Rua Vasco da Gama ☎ 967 023 840

QUARTEIRA
AquaShow

Combined waterpark and bird garden with a wax museum.

✉ On N396 just outside town ☎ 289 389 396; www.aquashowpark.com

SILVES
Aqualand

Another huge water park, Aqualand (formerly the Big One) is fully equipped with a variety of rides, tunnels and wave machines.

✉ N125, Alcantarilha ☎ 282 320 230; www.bigone-waterpark.com

VILAMOURA
Polvo

Company with several boats, offering luxury motor yachts, dolphin spotting trips and small boat charter.

✉ Vilamoura Marina ☎ 289 388 149

Best views

- Battlements of Monsaraz castle

- Cabo Espichel, at the tip of the Arrábida peninsula

- Casal dos Loivos, above Pinhão, Alto Douro

- Cliffs directly above Praia do Camilo, near Lagos, Algarve

- The dining room window of the Pousada da Rainha Santa Isabel at Estremoz

- Foia, above Monchique, Algarve

- Santa Luzia Basilica, Viana do Castelo

- Top of the Belém tower, Lisbon

- Torre, in the Serra da Estrela (mainland Portugal's highest mountain peak)

- Upper level of Dom Luis I bridge, Porto

Golf courses

Ammaia, Clube de Golfe de Marvão
18-holes with water hazards and some steep sections. Come on a week day and get the course pretty much to yourself.
✉ Quinta do Prado, S. Salvador de Aramenha, Marvão ☎ 245 993 755; www.marvaogolfe.com

Clube de Golfe do Estoril
Its 16th hole is considered by some to be Portugal's best.
✉ Av. da República, Estoril ☎ 214 680 054; www.portugalgolf.pt

Golfe Montebelo
18 holes set among pines, oaks and lakes backed by the Serra de Caramulo and Serra da Estrela mountains.
✉ Farminhão, Viseu ☎ 232 856 464; www.golfemontebelo.pt

Golfe de Ponte de Lima
Great views can be enjoyed from this 9-hole, par 71, course to the south of town.

✉ Quinta de Pias, Fornelos, Ponte de Lima ☎ 258 743 414; www.golfe-pontedelima.com

Golfe Praia d'El Rei
With views across the dunes to the Atlantic this course is part of the 5-star Praia d'El Rei golf and country club.

✉ Vale de Janelas, Óbidos ☎ 262 905 005; www.praia-del-rey.com

Oitavos Golfe
18-hole, par 71, Robert Trent Jones-designed course, considered to be among Europe's best.

✉ Quinta da Marinha, Cascais ☎ 214 860 600; www.quintadamarinha-oitavosgolfe.pt

The Old Course
Listed among Europe's top 100 golf courses.

✉ Vilamoura ☎ 289 310 341; www.vilamouragolf.com

Oporto Golf Club
The oldest course in the country with a challenging first hole set against the prevailing north wind.

✉ Paramos, Espinho ☎ 227 342 008; www.oportogolfclub.com

Vale da Pinta Golf
Characterized by its many bunkers and 1,500-year-old olive trees.

✉ Carvoeiro Golfe, Carvoeiro ☎ 282 340 900; www.pestanagolf.com

Vidago Palace Golf Club
South of Chaves this course offers 9 holes over hilly terrain, played over two rounds with a par of 33.

✉ Parque de Vidago, Vidago ☎ 276 999 404; www.vidagopalace.com

Best small towns and villages

Cacela Velha Perched on a bluff above the lagoons of the Ria Formosa, this tiny village, complete with cobbled streets and small chapel, is a fantastic place to watch the sunset over a cool beer and tapas.

Castelo de Vide One of the region's most lived-in, fortified hill towns, its attractive lower town, with large central square and monumental church, leads up into the medieval village with its winding cobbled lanes, gothic doorways and 13th-century Jewish quarter. Don't miss Portugal's oldest synagogue or Fonte da Vila.

Marvão Perched atop a granite crag, the village of Marvão (➤ 156) is undoubtedly one of Portugal's most impressive fortified hill towns. Its 13th-century castle and ramparts offer 360-degree views over the plains of the Alentejo and into Spain just 6km (3.7miles) away.

Monsanto Nestled on a hillside in the middle of a plain, this village has been built around huge granite boulders which often form part of the buildings themselves. Head to the top to see the 12th-century ruins of the castle and chapel.

Óbidos Undoubtedly one of Portugal's prettiest villages, with its whitewashed cottages hung with bright flowers and its cobbled lanes and squares (➤ 48–49). It was traditionally given to Portuguese queens as a wedding present.

Ponte de Lima This peaceful town sits on the banks of the River Lima, its medieval stone bridge leading to a pretty main square, fine buildings and shady riverside promenade. Make the most of the superb manor house accommodation to be found in the area.

Sintra Sintra is on most visitors' 'must see' list (➤ 132–133). Its cool climate and lush green forests made it the summer destination of choice for Portuguese kings and nobles. As a result it boasts several major palaces, convents and castles in addition to an exceptional collection of grand houses.

Sortelha This tiny hilltop hamlet has been fortified since the 13th century, its tiny granite houses built over and around giant boulders, with narrow lanes twisting between. Enjoy a great meal at the Restaurante Dom Sancho, just inside the main gate.

Tomar Built as the medieval headquarters of the Knights Templar and later passed to the Order of Christ, the castle and convent, with its elaborate cloisters, are Tomar's main attraction (➤ 134).

Valença do Minho Leave your car outside the ancient gates and wander into this massive, enclosed double fortress to enjoy the fantastic architecture, superb views over the Minho to Spain and some great textiles shops and outdoor cafés (➤ 102).

Peace and quiet

THE AVEIRO RIA

This great, brackish lagoon (commonly known as the Ria), joined to the sea by a narrow neck of water, spreads its finger-like inlets out across the flat, marshy land, extending 40km (25 miles) in total from Ovar, in the north, down to Mira, south of the sea mouth. The rich bird life to be seen here includes herons, egrets, wildfowl and abundant snipe and other waders.

A hump-backed bridge over the Ria north of Aveiro takes the N327 on to the long, narrow spit of sand dunes, pine woods and marshes between the Ria and the sea, leading up to Ovar. There are several places to stop and swim.

BERLENGA ISLANDS

Lying about 10km (6 miles) offshore and home to huge colonies of seabirds, these are the only islands off the coast of mainland Portugal. They can be visited on day trips from the port of Peniche, near Óbidos (➤ 48–49) between June and September. Shags, herring gulls and guillemots nest on the cliffs. It is possible to camp overnight or stay at the main island's basic hostel, open May–Sep (☎ 262 789 571 for details).

MONTESINHO NATURAL PARK

Up in the far, northeast corner of the country, this is Portugal at its most remote. The park begins just north of Bragança, and extends up to the mountains which form a natural border with Spain. This giant hump of wild and exposed upland, dotted with huge, ancient and magnificent chestnut trees, is richer in wildlife than anywhere else in the country. You may see hares leaping through the heather, and birds of prey hovering overhead. The plentiful wild boar are nocturnal and seldom seen; so are the packs of wolves, which can sometimes be heard howling on a winter's night.

PENEDA-GERÊS NATIONAL PARK
Bordering Spain in the far north of the country, these mountains include some of the wildest, most dramatic scenery Portugal has to offer. This is a gorse and boulder-strewn wilderness splintered by ravines and noisy streams, and fringed by granite peaks where buzzards and kestrels soar. There are waymarked walking trails and campsites within the park.

RIA FORMOSA NATURAL PARK
This is a protected area of wetlands, salt-marshes, lagoons and salt pans, around and extending east of Faro, the Algarve's capital. Public access is restricted for conservation reasons but there are several different points around the perimeter where birdwatchers can go to spot egrets, spoonbills and teal.

WEST COAST BEACHES
To escape the crowds basking on the Algarve's golden sand throughout the summer, head for the west coast. The sea is cooler and rougher, and it can be windy, but there is a genuine sense of isolation. The sandy beaches of Bordeira, Castelejo and Arrifana are the size of athletics stadiums, backed by cliffs sheltering them from the wind. A few serious surfers are attracted here by the great, white Atlantic rollers which break out to sea and rush in noisily. Further north, around Odeceixe, the sand softens to a sandy estuary of wetlands, populated by dazzling white egrets.

Exploring

Other than the Algarve, Lisbon area, Porto and a few other tourist spots, Portugal neither gets, nor expects, many visitors. Consequently, there are plenty of opportunities for people to get close to this beautiful country and its people.

In the lush, green Minho in the far north of the country, many a traveller has been overwhelmed by local hospitality – particularly people who have stayed in private homes under the *Turismo de Habitação* scheme.

Portugal offers true wilderness, too, in the remote Peneda-Gerês and Montesinho national parks, and in the wilds of the Serra da Estrela, the country's highest mountain range. Southwards, you need only drive a couple of hours from the Algarve's beach resorts to find the cork-forested plains of the Alentejo, sprinkled with dazzling white, Moorish-style villages.

Porto and the North

The north is the cradle of the nation, where the Kingdom of Portugal was proclaimed in the 12th century. The centre of power shifted south many centuries ago, though the North remains richly historic. Towns such as Guimarães and Coimbra have both, for short periods, been the national capital.

Porto

Scenically the region is extremely diverse, from the lush and fertile Minho, north of Porto, described as the Costa Verde (Green Coast), to the austere mountains of the Serra da Estrela and the grape-growing Douro valley. In between are the somnolent marshes and salt pans of the Aveiro lagoon.

The quintessential Portuguese conservatism is more evident in the north – even in Porto, the country's second city – than in the south.

PORTO

Portugal's second largest city has a history going back some 4,000 years, making it one of the oldest towns in Europe. As a booming industrial centre some people find it ugly. Others are quick to discover the charms of the old town and the wine-related treats of Vila Nova de Gaia's port lodges (▶ 54–55).

For most visitors Porto's heart is in its old town, on the north bank of the river. The area is coloured by dense clusters of tall, dilapidated, red-tiled houses thrown haphazardly together in what looks like an oversized village spilling down from the city centre to the Ribeira district on the River Douro quayside.

Alleys and walkways, some of them tortuously steep, wind through this labyrinth of homes and artisans' workshops; women in voluminous skirts sell fruit, vegetables and sardines, while washing lines overhead flap with white sheets and brightly coloured clothing. Far from being a sanitised old

town, as is found in so many European cities, this is a real living quarter, buzzing with activity.

Porto's ancient, rickety trams are a fun way to get around. Hop on one anywhere along the Douro quayside and it will take you along the river to its mouth. However, most sightseeing can be done within a fairly short walk of the city centre, though you do need stamina for the steep gradients.

🚩 2E

ℹ️ Rua Clube dos Fenianos 25 ☎ 223 393 470

Fundação Serralves

The Serralves Foundation museum of modern art is housed in a striking post-modernist building in the grounds of the 1930s art deco Casa de Serralves. There are some outstanding contributions by contemporary Portuguese artists, as well as works by Picasso and Warhol.

🚩 *Porto 1c (off map)* ✉️ Rua D João de Castro 210 ☎ 808 200 543 🕐 Tue–Thu 10–7, Fri–Sat 10–10, Sun 10–8

 Moderate

a walk around Porto

Starting at Estaçao de São Bento

Porto's central railway station is built on the foundations of Ave Maria convent, of which a few vestiges remain. Whether you are travelling by train or not, the station is worth visiting to see its fabulous collection of giant *azulejo* (tile) murals, depicting great events in the city's history.

Walk up the Avenida Dr Afonso Henriques to the Sé (Cathedral; ➤ 88).

The main doors of the Sé give on to a pedestrianized square from where a stone staircase leads down into the warren of alleys which is Porto's old town. Twist down through this labyrinth, to emerge on Rua Infante Dom Henrique.

Turn right along Rua Infante Dom Henrique to reach the Praça do Infante Dom Henriques.

Visit the Palácio da Bolsa (➤ 86) and the adjacent Igreja de São Francisco (➤ 86).

Walk back along Rua Infante Dom Henrique to the Feitoria Inglesa.

This fine 18th-century town house is a 'factory' in the old-fashioned sense of a meeting

place of 'factors' or merchants rather than a manufacturing operation. It is now the headquarters of the British Association of Port Shippers, and the interior can only be visited by invitation from a member.

Turn right and follow the Rua de São João down to the Praça da Ribeira square, leading on to the Cais da Ribeira.

The Cais da Ribeira are at the heart of the tourist area with restaurants, cafés, shops and an open air market. The vista across the river to Vila Nova da Gaia, with the double-decker Dom Luis I bridge looming large a little way upstream, is spectacular.

Follow the quay up to the bridge, continuing for a few metres along Avenida Gustave Eiffel, then climb the long stone staircase up to the Avenida de Vimara Peres, emerging by the Dom Luis Bridge at its upper level.

Distance 3km (2 miles)
Time 2–5 hours, depending on length of visits
Start point São Bento Station
✚ *Porto 3a*
End point Upper level, Dom Luis Bridge ✚ *Porto 4c*
Lunch Taberna do Bebobos (€€)
✉ Cais da Ribeira 24 ☎ 222 053 565

Igreja de São Francisco

The Church of St Francis is one of the most amazing churches in Portugal, and to most tastes infinitely more beautiful than the Sé. Dazzling and intricate gilt work extends from ceiling to floor; it is said that there are over 400kg (880 pounds) of pure gold inside.

✚ Porto 2c ✉ Rua Infante D Henrique ⏰ Feb–May daily 9–6; Jul–Aug daily 9–8; Jun, Sep–Oct daily 9–7; Nov–Jan daily 9–5:30 ✋ Inexpensive

Museu de Soares dos Reis

Porto's principal museum occupies an 18th-century neo-classical house, which later served as the headquarters of the Napoleonic forces during the Peninsular War. It is said that Wellington and his officers, having defeated the French and ousted Marshall Soult in 1809, ate their dinner here. The spectacle was probably rather more arresting than this somewhat down-at-heel museum, which displays 19th- and early 20th-century Portuguese art.

✚ Porto 1a (off map) ✉ Rua de Dom Manuel II ☎ 22 339 3770 ⏰ Wed–Sun 10–6, Tue 2–6. Closed public hols ✋ Inexpensive. Free Sun until 2pm

Palácio da Bolsa

The fine 19th-century granite and marble palace once housed the city's parliament and judiciary as well as the stock exchange. The guided tour of the palace takes you from echoing hall to sumptuous salon. It includes exhibits illustrating the history of Porto, and makes an excellent introduction to the city. The star attraction is the amazing Arab Room, decorated in brilliant Moorish style with gilding, stained-glass windows, painted stucco and a pastiche of the Alhambra in Granada, Spain.

www.palaciodabolsa.pt

✚ Porto 2c ✉ Rua Ferreira Borges ☎ 223 399 000 ⏰ Apr–Oct daily 9–7; Nov–Mar 9–1, 2–6 ✋ Moderate 🍴 Many restaurants and cafés in the nearby Ribeira

Sé

Porto's austere, grey cathedral, where King João I and Philippa of Lancaster were married in 1387, dates from the 12th century, when it was a fortress as well as a place of worship. This explains the presence of granite battlements around the cloisters and forbidding square towers flanking the façade. The interior was completely re-vamped in baroque style during the 17th and 18th centuries. The two traditions sit rather inharmoniously together, and it is hard to describe the overall effect as either beautiful or inspiring. Don't miss the Romanesque rose window in the main western façade, or the lovely *azulejos* (tiles) round the cloisters.

➕ *Porto 3b* ✉ Terreiro da Sé ☎ 222 059 028 ◷ Church Nov–Mar Mon–Sat 8:45–12:30, 2:30–6, Sun and public hols 8:30–12:30, 2:30–6; Apr–Oct Mon–Sat 8:45–12:30, 2:30–7, Sun and public hols 8:30–12:30, 2:30–7. Cloisters Nov–Mar Mon–Sat 9–12:15, 2.30–5:15, Sun and public hols 2:30–5:15; Apr–Oct Mon–Sat 9–12:15, 2:30–6, Sun and public hols 2:30–6 ✋ Church free; cloisters inexpensive ❓ Occasional classical concerts

Torre dos Clérigos

The soaring, rocket-like 75m-high (245ft) granite tower of the Igreja dos Clérigos has been a main feature of the Porto skyline since the building was completed in 1749. The exhausting climb to the top is up a spiral staircase of 225 worn steps, and is rewarded by fabulous views over the city, or severe vertigo, or both.

➕ *Porto 2a* ✉ Rua S Filipe de Nery ☎ 222 001 729 ◷ Church Nov–Mar Mon–Sat 9–12, 3:30–7:30, Sun 10–1, 8:30–10:30; Apr–Oct Mon–Sat 9–12, 3:30–7:30, Sun 10–1, 9–10. Tower Nov–Mar daily 10–12, 2–7; Apr–Jul, Sep–Oct daily 9:30–1, 2–7; Aug daily 10–7 ✋ Inexpensive

Vila Nova de Gaia

Best places to see, pages 54–55.

More to see in the North

AMARANTE

Amarante is an enchanting little town which sits beside the Tâmega river, spanned by the photogenic 18th-century São Gonçalo bridge of honey-coloured granite. Terraces and verandahs overlook the willow-lined water where anglers cast for trout. A tiled cupola rises above the mellow stone of the 16th-century **São Gonçalo convent.** Inside is the tomb of São Gonçalo himself; votive offerings are left in the Chapel of Miracles.

Next to the church, part of the convent has been converted into **Museu Municipal Amadeo de Souza-Cardoso** (museum of modern art), devoted to the works of local artists, with many works by Souzo-Cardoso.

✚ 3D ✉ 56km (35 miles) east of Porto ❓ Colourful festival on first weekend Jun

São Gonçalo Church

🕐 Cloisters: Tue–Sun 10–12, 2–5 ✋ Free

Museu Municipal Amadeo de Souza-Cardoso

✉ Alameda Teixeira da Pascoaes ☎ 225 420 272 🕐 Tue–Fri 9–12:30, 2–5, Sat–Sun 10–12:30, 2–5 ✋ Inexpensive

AVEIRO

The 'Venice of Portugal' sits on the edge of the great Ria and is sliced through by three canals, each spanned by arched bridges. Aveiro's wealth was in fishing, salt-panning and the gathering of *molico* water weed – a rich, natural fertilizer. The brightly painted *moliceiro* boats with high, curved bows are of Phoenician ancestry and although chemical fertilizers have taken much of the trade, *molico* is still a prized natural resource, gathered with long rakes. By the late 16th century the town was an important port, but gradually declined as the coastal sand banks closed the lagoon's sea mouth. In 1808, the sandbar was breached with explosives and the traditional industries were rekindled, though never to their earlier level.

➕ 2G ✉ 52km (32 miles) south of Porto ❓ Aveiro holds a major festival at the end of August (dates variable), with *moliceiro* boat races

ℹ Rua João Mendonça 8 ☎ 234 420 760

BARCELOS

Barcelos stages the largest weekly agricultural fair and market in the north of Portugal. Bartering begins at dawn every Thursday in the expansive Campo da República square which, from Friday to Wednesday, appears out of all proportion to this small, rural town. By mid-morning Barcelos is a riot of trading with crates of chickens and rabbits; truckfuls of cattle, sheep and pigs; crude pottery including the famous cockerels in dozens of different sizes, and cherubic-looking monks dressed in black robes with strings attached which, when pulled, may shock the unsuspecting; huge piles of fruit and vegetables; CDs whose vendors try to blast each other out of contention with tinny decks running on car batteries; and clothes ranging from rustic berets to real leather bomber jackets.

   The town is worth a brief stop on non-market days to see the enormous square centred by a beautiful fountain.

✛ 2D ✉ 20km (12.5 miles) west of Braga ❓ As well as the Thursday market, there is a major religious festival, the *Festa das Cruzes*, on 3 May

ℹ Largo da Porta Nova ☎ 253 811882

BRAGA

Braga is sometimes known as the 'Portuguese Rome'. The town is the religious capital of Portugal. At times during Portuguese history, the Church has wielded more power than the monarchy or government with Braga at the centre of this influence. Since the revolution of 1974 the ecclesiastic and political establishments have had less to do with each other, but Portugal is still a strongly spiritual nation and Braga's Holy Week celebrations in particular (➤ 24) are a striking testament to the depth of religious feeling here.

There are 80 churches in this town, of which only the **Sé** (Cathedral) is unmissable. The foundations are 12th-century, with the main west door and the whole southern portal the most obvious visible survivors of the original Romanesque buildings. There are Gothic, Renaissance, baroque and Manueline among an extraordinary diversity of styles which somehow come together

into a harmonious whole. Most striking is a pair of ornate gilt 18th-century organs adorned with cherubs, dolphins and mermaids. In the Capela de São Pedro (St Peter's Chapel) are some outstanding *azulejos* by the master tile artist António Oliveira Bernardes; also not to be missed is a beautiful fresco of the Virgin in the

Gothic Capela de São Geraldo (St Gerald's Chapel) and the Capela dos Reis (Chapel of the Kings) containing the tombs of Dom Henriques and Dona Teresa, whose son, Dom Afonso Henriques, became the first king of Portugal.

The pick of Braga's other sites are the Capela dos Coimbras (Coimbras Chapel) on Rua do Soto with its flamboyant Manueline tower and, inside, *azulejos* depicting the story of Adam and Eve; the splendid 17th-century baroque Igreja Santa Cruz (Holy Cross Church) on Rua do Anjo; and the extensive Antigo Paço Espiscopal (former Archbishop's Palace) with its peaceful, well-tended Santa Barbara gardens and Largo do Paco courtyard.

Three kilometres (2 miles) outside Braga is an ornate baroque terraced staircase of more than 1,000 steps leading to the Bom Jesus sanctuary.

www.cm-braga.pt

✚ 2C ✉ 52km (32 miles) northeast of Porto

ℹ Praça da República

☎ 253 262 550

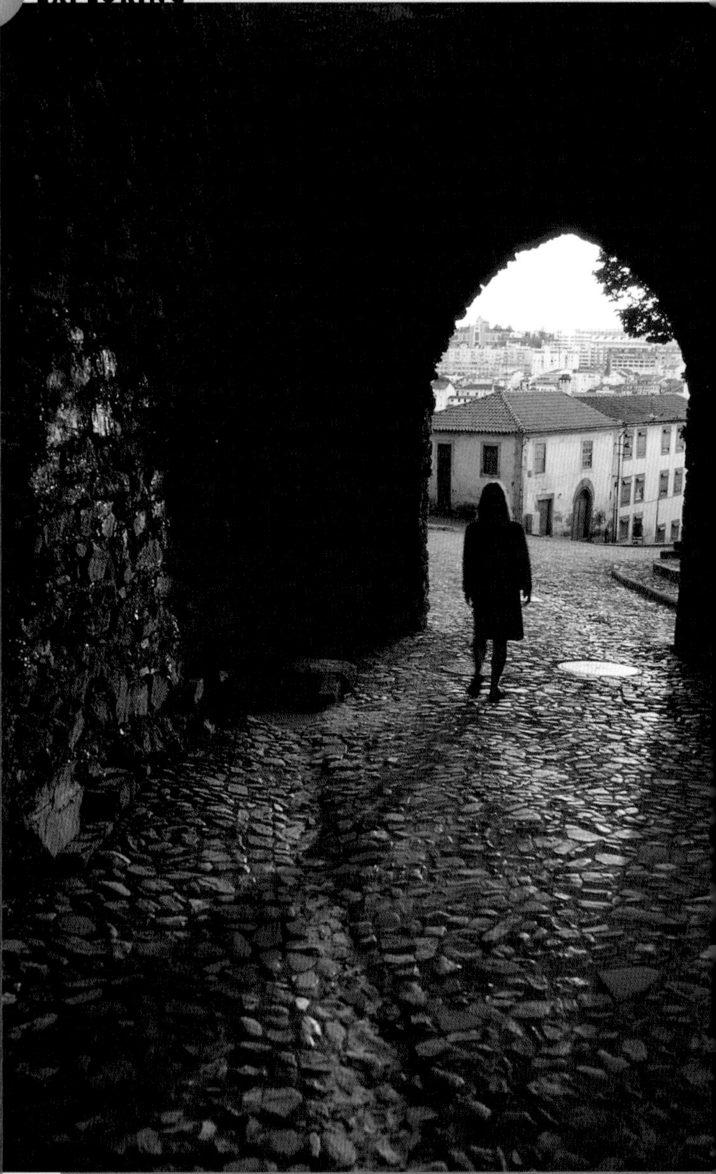

BRAGANÇA

Up in the northeast of Portugal and cut off from the rest of the country by three mountain ranges, Bragança stands alone. Yet behind this remoteness is a city with an illustrious past: it has been fought over from prehistoric times through to the 19th-century Peninsular War, with sieges, battles and invasions turning on control of the walled citadel and its grey stone ramparts. The dukedom of Bragança became the royal house of Portugal, and supplied England with a queen, when Charles II married Catherine of Bragança.

There are bustling fruit, vegetable and grain markets distracting attention from the stately churches and fading, grandiose buildings of another era. Steep cobbled lanes lead up to the gates of the citadel and castle walls, within which everyday life goes on around the soaring Gothic keep. Washing hangs drying outside cottages with red-tiled roofs, haphazardly thrown together. Children play and chickens scratch about the vegetable plots and rubbish heaps, creating an almost medieval atmosphere.

Bragança is dominated by its forbidding and seemingly impenetrable **castle.** A tall keep is surrounded by crenellated turrets, with only narrow slits letting in any light. Fittingly, it houses a **Military Museum** charting the history of Portugal at war, with emphasis on the African colonies. From a platform at the top of the keep, there are wonderful views over the town and mountains.

Catherine of Bragança married English King Charles II. Her dowry included the Portuguese trading post of Bombay, and she introduced to England the custom of taking afternoon tea.

www.cm-braganca.pt

➕ 6C ✉ 253km (157 miles) northeast of Porto

ℹ Avenida Cidade de Zamora ☎ 273 381 273

Castle and Military Museum

🕐 Fri–Wed 9–12, 2–5. Closed public hols 💶 Inexpensive

COIMBRA

Set on a steep hill rising from the north bank of
the River Mondego, Coimbra is one of the
oldest university towns in Europe. It was also
the capital of Portugal in the 12th and 13th
centuries, after Guimarães and before Lisbon.
Curiously, however, this concentration of
historic buildings, romantically set on a hill
overlooking the river, makes few concessions
to tourism. The atmosphere varies between
lively and youthful in term time, and stuffy and
museum-like during vacations.

The **Velha Universidade** (Old University) of Coimbra was
founded in 1290. Up at the highest point of the city is the
institution's main courtyard, enclosed by a great ceremonial hall
with a superb, 17th-century painted ceiling; the gloriously
flamboyant, Manueline São Miguel chapel; and a small Museum of
Sacred Art. The most splendid building in Coimbra, however, is the
university library, which is composed of three glittering 18th-
century baroque rooms with vast expanses of gilded wood. These
have many Oriental features, reflecting the Age of Discoveries.

The Sé Velha (the Old Cathedral) is a beautiful Romanesque
church with many more recent features, begun in the late 12th
century after Coimbra had become capital of the new Kingdom of
Portugal. There is a beautiful altarpiece and some fine Renaissance
side chapels, but somehow it is the deeply moving ambience of
the cathedral which is the true attraction.

Down in the 'new' town is Coimbra's other great architectural
jewel, the **Mosteiro da Santa Cruz** (Monastery of the Holy
Cross). Like the cathedral, it was founded in the 12th century by
Afonso Henriques, first king of Portugal, since which time it has
been liberally endowed with embellishments. The most interesting
features are the ornate, carved stone pulpit in the centre of the
church; the Manueline choir, where the voyages of Vasco da Gama

are depicted in gilt wood carvings; and the sacristy, with its collection of Renaissance art.

About 17km (10.5 miles) south of Coimbra is **Conimbriga,** the largest Roman archaeological site in Portugal. Less than a quarter of the site has been excavated, but it is worth visiting to see the superb mosaic floors that survive.

www.cm-coimbra.pt

🚩 2H ✉ 150km (93 miles) northeast of Lisbon

ℹ Largo da Portagem (☎ 239 488 120)

University buildings

☎ 239 859 800 🕐 Nov–Mar daily tickets 9:30–5, visits 10–5:30; Apr–Oct daily tickets 8:30–7, visits 9–7:30 🖐 Moderate

Monastery of the Holy Cross

✉ Praça 8 de Maio 🕐 Mon–Sat 9–12, 2–5, Sun 4–5 🖐 Inexpensive

Conimbriga ruins

✉ South of Coimbra, at Condeixa-a-Nova 🕐 Ruins Oct–May daily 10–6; Jun–Sep daily 9–8. Museum Oct–May Tue–Sun 10–6; Jun–Sep Tue–Sun 10–8 🖐 Inexpensive

FIGUEIRA DA FOZ

Figueira da Foz is a fishing port and small beach holiday resort at the mouth of the River Mondego. The chief attraction is the enormous beach; the great Atlantic breakers are popular with surfers, although the rough sea can disappoint families who come hoping to swim. The town has several modern holiday hotels, discos, a casino and tennis courts.

www.figueiraturismo.com

✚ 1H ✉ 42km (26 miles) west of Coimbra

ℹ Avenida 25 de Abril ☎ 233 402 827

GUIMARÃES

In 1139 Afonso Henriques was declared the first king of Portugal, and made Guimarães his capital. Although the centre of power soon shifted south – first to Coimbra and later to Lisbon – Guimarães still has a historic kernel,

reached beyond the sprawl of textile and shoe factories which make it an important and prosperous industrial centre.

The ruined 10th-century **castle** stands rather dramatically on a rocky hill in the middle of town. There are seven great towers surrounding the keep, but otherwise little to see other than the great views over Guimarães and the surrounding countryside from the ramparts, which can be easily climbed.

The **Paço dos Duques** (Palace of the Dukes of Braganza) is the principal monument and museum to Guimarães's status as the cradle of the Portuguese nation. A fine, bronze statue of Afonso Henriques stands outside, guarding the four sturdy buildings with massive corner towers, built by Dom Afonso, the first Duke of Bragança. Inside, the unmissable rooms are the banqueting hall with its splendid wooden ceiling, and a fine collection of Persian carpets and Flemish tapestries.

www.guimaraesturismo.com

✚ 2D ✉ 49km (30 miles) northeast of Porto

ℹ Alameda de São Damaso ☎ 253 412 450

Castle

🕐 Daily 9:30–12:30, 2–5:30

Paço dos Duques

☎ 253 412 273 🕐 Jun–Sep Tue–Sun 9:30–6:30; Oct–May Tue–Sun 9:30–12, 2–5 ♿ Moderate; free Sun am

LUSO

The still, fresh mineral water of the famous Luso spa is favoured all over Portugal. It has a high level of radioactivity, which may sound alarming but is, apparently, beneficial. Certainly, many Portuguese regard the waters of Luso as a panacea; liver complaints in particular are reported to be eased at the very mention of a drop of Luso water. The Buçaco Palace Hotel once described itself in a brochure as 'the shadiest hotel in Portugal'. This was actually a reference to the

hotel's beautiful walled forest of oak, cork, pine and rare imported exotic trees (which do indeed provide a deep shade).

➕ 2G ✉ 25km (15.5 miles) northeast of Coimbra

🛈 Rua Emídio Navarro ☎ 231 939 133

SERRA DO CARAMULO

Caramulo is the main town in the Serra do Caramulo, a range of rolling inland mountains little visited by foreign tourists, but an excellent stop for motorists taking a hinterland route between north and south. The town of Caramulo itself is on the edge of the Cambarinho Natural Park, in which rare forms of oleander are conserved, amid vineyards and cattle pasture. The town has a small *pousada* (state-run hotel) and two museums – one housing a collection of vintage cars, the other ancient and modern art, including works by Dalí and Picasso.

www.serra-caramulo.com

➕ 2G ✉ 40km (25 miles) southwest of Viseu

Museu do Caramulo

☎ 232 861270 🕐 Jul–Sep daily 10–1, 2–6; Oct–Jun until 5 💰 Moderate

SERRA DA ESTRÊLA

Best places to see, pages 50–51.

VALENÇA DO MINHO

Looking across the Minho towards Tuy, its Spanish counterpart, the border town of Valença do Minho has for centuries been on Portugal's front line of defence. Two massive sets of ramparts protect the old town, which is entered via a drawbridge; inside are narrow cobbled streets and a lively atmosphere with large numbers of shops, patronized by Spaniards who have crossed the frontier to sniff out the best bargains. There are great views across to Spain from the walls, which can be walked around, and from the *pousada* set into the ramparts. The new town, at the bottom of the hill outside the walls, has little of interest.

✚ 1C ✉ 52km (32 miles) north of Viana do Castelo and 108km (67 miles) north of Porto 🕐 Unrestricted access to the walls
ℹ Avenida de Espanha ☎ 251 823 374

VIANA DO CASTELO

This attractive fishing port, and venue for the greatest *festa* in the north of Portugal each August, stands on the north bank of the Lima estuary, dominated by the lusciously wooded Santa Luzia mountain. The beautiful Praça da República is surrounded by fine houses decorated with Manueline embellishments dating from the 16th and 17th centuries, when the town became prosperous on trade and fishing from the Grand Banks of Newfoundland, and exporting wine to Britain.

Viana is delightful to wander around and has a strong folkloric tradition; on Sundays and saints' days, people frequently wear traditional regional dress – the men in bright waistcoats and black, broad-brimmed hats, the women in embroidered skirts and head scarves.

A narrow 4km (2.5-mile) road winds up to the basilica and hotel on Monte de Santa Luzia, from where the views are sensational. On a clear day the coastline can be traced from the Minho and Spain beyond, most of the way down to Porto.

✚ 1C ✉ 56km (35 miles) north of Porto ❓ Viana stages northern Portugal's

greatest *romaria* and *festa*, Nossa
Senhora da Agonía, over the weekend
nearest to 15 August
🛈 Rua do Hospital Velho (off Praça de
Erva) ☎ 258 822 620

VISEU

Viseu is a solemn town of dignified airs at the heart of Dão wine-producing country. Its history is centred on Vasco Fernandes (1480–1543), later styled Grão Vasco – the 'Great Vasco' – founder of the Viseu school of painting. As he was one of the most eminent painters in Portuguese history, and the one principally responsible for introducing the Renaissance to the country, his adopted home town, Viseu, is naturally proud of him. So there is a Grão Vasco museum, a Grão Vasco hotel, and Grão Vasco wine – one of the most famous brands of Dão.

The **Museu de Grão Vasco** is housed in the Bishop's Palace opposite the Cathedral. Many of Grão Vasco's most famous works are exhibited, including his interpretations of St Peter and St Sebastian. The museum also contains work by Gaspar Vaz, another Portuguese master, and some beautiful 16th-century *azulejos*.

The twin-towered Cathedral was built in a hotch-potch of different styles, between the 13th and 18th centuries, and is worth seeing. Most remarkable are the gilded, baroque altarpiece, and the Renaissance cloisters, decorated with 18th-century *azulejos*.

✚ 3F ✉ 81km (50 miles) southeast of Porto

🛈 Avenida Calouste Gulbenkian ☎ 232 420 950

Museu de Grão Vasco

☎ 232 422 049 🕒 Tue 2–6, Wed–Sun 10–6. Closed public hols

✋ Moderate. Free Sun morning

HOTELS

ALIJÓ
Pousada Barão de Forrester (€€€)

Superb *pousada* surrounded by port vineyards.

✉ Rua José Rufino ☎ 259 959 215; www.pousadas.pt

AMARES
Pousada Santa Maria do Bouro (€€€)

This converted Cistercian monastery is one of the most historic Portuguese *pousadas*. The architectural lines have been matched by elegant décor, especially in the vast stone dining room.

✉ 4720–688 Amares ☎ 235 371 970; www.pousadas.pt

ARCOS DE VALDEVEZ
Casa da Ponte (€€)

Late 17th-century country mansion next to the River Vez offering the perfect quiet retreat for walking and boat trips and ideally placed for touring the far north.

✉ Rua dos Milagres 78 ☎ 258 516 107; www.adere-pg.pt

BARCELOS
Quinta do Convento da Franqueira (€€)

A beautiful Turismo de Habitacão in a sea of *vinho verde* vineyards, next to a ruined monastery about 5km (3 miles) from Barcelos. The English owners rent just three rooms. Booking essential.

✉ Pereira ☎ 253 831 606; www.quintadafranqueira.com

BRAGA
Hotel do Parque (€€)

A fine old hotel with a very friendly and comfortable atmosphere.

✉ Parque de Bom Jesus do Monte ☎ 253 603 479

Hotel Residencial D Sofia (€)

Refurbished hotel set on a quiet square in the city. Reasonably sized rooms make a good base for budget travellers.

✉ Largo de São João do Souto 131 ☎ 253 263 160

BRAGANÇA
Pousada de São Bartolomeu (€€€)
This modern *pousada*, which has the added advantage of wonderful views over the castle and town, offers good quality accommodation with an on-site restaurant.

✉ Estrada do Turismo, 5300–271 Bragança ☎ 273 331 493

COIMBRA
Bragança (€€)
A wonderfully located hotel that is packed with good, old-fashioned charm.

✉ Largo das Ameias 10 ☎ 239 822 171; www.hotelbraganca.com

Quinta das Lágrimas (€€€)
Travellers who want to get away from the hustle and bustle can enjoy a relaxed stay in this peaceful, quaint old house or its modern new wing.

✉ Rua António Augusto Gonçalves, Santa Clara ☎ 239 802 380; www.quintadaslagrimas.com

GÊRES
Pousada São Bento (€€–€€€)
The beautiful location of this mountain chalet amid a forested national park offers superb views and excellent hiking.

✉ 4850–047 Caniçada ☎ 253 649 150; www.pousadas.pt

GUIMARÃES
Pousada de Santa Marinha da Costa (€€€)
A richly atmospheric *pousada* in a converted monastery.

✉ Largo Domingos Leite de Castro, Lugar de Castro ☎ 253 511 249; www.pousadas.pt

MESÃO FRIO
Pousada Solar de Rede (€€€)
Perfect location for touring the Douro Valley, this fine restored 18th-century mansion is set in large manicured gardens.

✉ Santa Christina ☎ 254 890 130; www.pousadas.pt

PORTO

Albergaria Miradouro (€€)
A comfortable, friendly place in the same building as the
penthouse Portucale restaurant, one of Porto's best.
✉ Rua da Alegria 598 ☎ 225 370 717; www.miradouro-portucale.com

Boa Vista (€€)
This is Porto's *only* hotel with a sea view. Small and charming,
though out of the way at Foz do Douro.
✉ Esplanada do Castelo 58 ☎ 225 320 020; www.hotelboavista.com

Infante de Sagres (€€€)
Porto's only grand, sumptuous, old-style hotel. Antique-stuffed
rooms and immaculate service.
✉ Praça Dona Filipa de Lencastre 62 ☎ 223 398 500;
www.hotelinfantesagres.pt

Malaposta (€)
In a convenient location, Malaposta offers a chic modern interior.
✉ Rua da Conceição 80 ☎ 222 006 278; www.hotelmalposta.com

Pestana Porto (€€€)
On the Praça de Ribiera overlooking the river and quayside at Vila
Gaia, on the doorstep of the best bars and restaurants in town.
✉ Praça da Ribeira 1 ☎ 223 402 300; www.pestana.com

VALENÇA DO MINHO
Pousada de São Teotónio (€€–€€€)
Peaceful location with views over the Mihno river, this *pousada*
sits inside the walls of the old fort.
✉ 4930–619 Valença do Minho ☎ 251 800 260; www.pousadas.pt

VIANA DO CASTELO
Pousada do Monte de Santa Luzia (€€–€€€)
Famous old hotel, now a *pousada*. Amazing views over the
Minho coast.
✉ Monte de Santa Luzia ☎ 258 800 370; www.pousadas.pt

VILA NOVA DE CERVEIRA
Pousada Dom Dinis (€€€)
This beautiful 13th-century manor house is one of Portugal's smaller *pousadas*. Each room has its own courtyard.
✉ 4920–296 Vila Nova de Cerveira ☎ 251 708 120; www.pousadas.pt

RESTAURANTS

AMARANTE
Adega Regional Kilowatt (€)
Artisan-produced air-dried ham in country bread accompanied by glasses of *vinho verde* is all this tiny rustic eatery serves.
✉ Rua 31 de Janeiro ☎ 255 433159 🕐 Closed Mon usually Oct–May

Zé da Calçada (€€)
Some think this restaurant overpriced for its good though not outstanding food. But the view over the stone bridge and town are superlative and a treat to savour.
✉ Rua 31 de Janeiro ☎ 255 426 814

BARCELOS
Casa dos Arcos (€)
Good homey cooking with excellent bread and fish. Don't even think of coming without making a reservation if it is a Thursday (market day).
✉ Rua Duques de Bragança 158 ☎ 253 811 975 🕐 Closed Mon

BRAGA
Pousada de Amares (€€)
The exceptional vaulted stone dining room makes an atmospheric place to eat excellent regional Minho cuisine.
✉ Amares (north of Braga) ☎ 253 371 970

BRAGANÇA
Lá em Casa (€€)
Best place in town to eat. *Lá em casa* means 'at home'. Bearing this in mind, the fish and meat dishes are surprisingly elaborate.
✉ Rua Marques de Pombal 7 ☎ 273 322111

COIMBRA
Cozinha (€)
Cosy, exceptionally friendly and family-run. Homey Portuguese cooking including top-notch *bacalhau Gomes de Sá* (sliced and served with potatoes and hard boiled eggs).

✉ Rua Azeiteiras 65 ☎ 239 823 115 🕐 Closed Sun

Zé Manel (€€)
The atmosphre is jaunty and studenty during the academic term, and the restaurant remains popular, though more sedately so, during vacation time. The *cabrito* (goat) is excellent.

✉ Beco do Forno 12 ☎ 239 823 790 🕐 Closed Sat evening and Sun

GUIMARÃES
Vira Bar/Restaurant (€€)
This modern wine bar/restaurant set in a historic town house has a relaxing ambience. Portuguese and international dishes.

✉ Largo Condessa do Juncal 27 ☎ 253 518 427 🕐 Closed Sun and Mon

PORTO
Café Majestic (€)
A wonderful 18th-century gilt and mirrored city centre café. Perfect for a snack lunch.

✉ Rua de Santa Catarina 112 ☎ 222 003 887

Filha da Mãe Preta (€€)
Richly atmospheric and mildly raunchy restaurant on the quayside. If you are brave enought to risk trying *tripas à Portuguesa* (tripe with beans), this is the best place to do it.

✉ Cais da Ribeira 40 ☎ 222 086 066

Ora Viva (€€)
Quaint restaurant one street back from the riverside. The menu concentrates on seafood.

✉ Rua Fonte Taurina 83 ☎ 222 052 033 🕐 Closed Mon

Portucale (€€€)
Superb views can be enjoyed from the penthouse plus top-notch
international cuisine and modern interpretations of traditional
dishes.
✉ Rua da Alegria 598 ☎ 225 370 717

Postigo do Carvão (€)
Traditional *bacalhau* (salted cod) and seafood with rice are
specialities here along with other Portuguese dishes. There's
regular live music.
✉ Rua Fonte Taurina 24–34 ☎ 222 004 539

Taverna de Bebobos (€€)
Traditional Porto and Minho fare down on the quayside. A long
established restaurant, but now very popular with tourists.
✉ Cais da Ribeira 24–25 ☎ 222 053 565 ⊘ Closed Sun

VALENÇA DO MINHO
Pousada de São Teotónio (€€)
For your first or last meal in Portugal coming from, or *en route* to,
Spain, have it here with views across the Minho. Excellent regional
cuisine.
☎ 251 800 260

Vila Real
Espadeiro (€€)
Vila Real's top restaurant, which serves excellent *bacalhau*, trout
and suckling pig. There is also an extensive wine list.
✉ Avenida Almeida Lucena ☎ 259 322 302 ⊘ Closed Mon

SHOPPING

HANDICRAFTS AND SOUVENIRS
Centro de Artesanato de Barcelos
Excellent selection of local handicrafts and pottery, including the
famed Barcelos cockerels.
✉ Largo da Porta Nova, Barcelos ☎ 253 811 882

Ribeira Craft Centre
Very touristy but a comprehensive selection of artefacts from rugs to ceramics, mainly from the Minho and elsewhere in the north.
✉ Rua da Reboleira 37, Porto ☎ 223 320 076

MARKETS
Barcelos
One of the largest and most famous markets in Portugal.
🕔 Thu

Espinho
A large market selling handicrafts, ceramics, clothes and food.
✉ 19km (12 miles) south of Porto 🕔 Mon

Ponte de Lima
A colourful market in the Minho.
✉ Alternate Mon

Porto
The colourful, covered Bolhão market sells food and handicrafts.
✉ Corner of Rua Formosa and Rua da Sá de Bandeira 🕔 Mon–Fri

PORCELAIN AND CERAMICS
Painéis de Azulejos João Faustino
Exceptional quality panels of *azulejos* in traditional style and pattern.
✉ Rua Principal 30, Cumeira de Cima, Juncal, Porto de Mós ☎ 262 507 376

Vista Alegre
The famous porcelain manufacturer's main outlet in the city.
✉ Rua Cândido dos Reis 6, Porto ☎ 222 004 554

WINE
Solar do Vinho do Porto
If you haven't stocked up on port over the bridge in the lodges of Vila Nova de Gaia, here's another chance.
✉ Quinta da Maceirinha, Rua de Entre Quintas 220, Porto ☎ 226 094 749

ENTERTAINMENT

CASINOS
Casino da Póvoa
✉ Avenida Braga, Póvoa de Varim ☎ 252 690 888

Casino Solverde
✉ Rua 19, 85, Espinho

DISCOS AND NIGHTCLUBS
Scotch Club
Long established club in this buzzing university city.
✉ Quinta da Ínsua,Santa Clara, Coimbra

Swing
Throbbing nightclub where Porto's trendiest hang out.
✉ Rua de Julio Dinis 766, Porto ☎ 226 090 019

Via Latina
A noisy nightclub which plays techno music.
✉ Rua Almeida Garrett 1, Coimbra

Vinyl
Latest avant-garde sounds
✉ Avenida Afonso Henriques 43, Coimbra

FADO
Diligência
A bar where *fado* (Portugal's soul music) is often performed,
particularly during the summer academic term.
✉ Rua Nova 30, Coimbra ☎ 239 827667

Mal Cozinhado
A convivial restaurant on the Ribeira, which is also Porto's top
fado venue.
✉ Rua Outeirinho 13, Porto ☎ 22 208 1319

Lisbon and Central Portugal

As Portugal's capital city, Lisbon (Lisboa) holds a concentration of historical and cultural attractions and is the nation's most cosmopolitan city by far. Standing roughly halfway between north and south, it is also strategically placed for exploring the central regions of Estremadura and Ribatejo.

Lisboa
□

Estremadura is a region of rocky coast and flat plains, flanked by gentle hills to the north and south, and sprinkled with historic towns such as Sintra and Alcobaça.

The Ribatejo region to the northwest of Lisbon is less culturally rich. However, as it encompasses the flood-plain of the Tagus, its fecundity lies in the alluvial soil, allowing wheat and rice to be grown, and horses and cattle to graze on fertile pastures. The only place of great historical note in Ribatejo is Tomar, where the Order of Christ, successors of the crusading Knights Templar, had their base.

LISBON

If you are fit, the steep gradients of the hills over which central Lisbon is scattered are best explored on foot. The most famous part of town is the Alfama district, a labyrinth of cobbled alleys, miniature squares and whitewashed houses, rising in tiers from the Tagus. The architectural contrast with the nearby, low-lying Baixa district, which was totally destroyed in the devastating earthquake of 1755, is dramatic. This area was rebuilt in precise grid form with magnificent squares and avenues.

Another popular district is the Bairro Alto. This is the most bohemian quarter of the city, rising to the west in steep streets and stone staircases, and lined with restaurants, *fado* houses and mildly raffish bars. The lower part of the district, from which several lifts (elevators) rise to the upper reaches, is the elegant Chiado, with fashionable department stores and tea houses.

Westwards along the Tagus, the other area of Lisbon not to be missed is Belém. This home to some of Lisbon's finest Manueline architecture, evoking Portugal's great era of world discovery.

✚ 8T

🛈 Rua do Arsenal 15 ☎ 210 312 700

Alfama

Tumbling down the hillside from the Castelo de São Jorge to the Tagus is Lisbon's oldest district, the Alfama. Though inhabited by Greeks, Romans and Visigoths it was the Moors who left the most visible mark bere by way of its labyrinthine street plan aimed at deterring invaders. The best way to explore the winding lanes and miniature squares is definitely by foot. Start at the Sé, then head uphill past a couple of great *miradouros* (viewpoints) before cutting down past the Igreja de São Vicente to get lost amid the tiny houses with Moorish latticed shutters and flapping washing. Be sure to take your camera.

✚ *Lisboa 5b*

Baixa

Rebuilt after the catastrophic earthquake of 1755 by the first minister, the Marquês de Pombal, the Baixa district is a showpiece

of 18th-century architecture and is today the heart of the capital. Taking his influence from Paris, Pombal redesigned this central area immediately behind the river along a Classical grid-plan, including monumental squares and fine symmetrical façades.

Lisbon's main gateway in the 18th-century was via the River Tagus from the sea, and Pombal was eager to create an impression of grandeur, worthy of Portugal's glorious past and equal to any in Europe. The vast, three-sided Praça do Comércio did exactly this with its three imperious, arcaded façades opening directly onto the Tagus. The square's elaborate triumphal arch leads up the decoratively cobbled Rua Augusta, past Classical buildings and shopfronts, into the recently restored Praça Dom Pedro IV —or Rossio. In the middle stands the statue of Dom Pedro IV, which, in fact, started out life as Maximilian of Mexico. Cast in France and on its way to Mexico, the statue was docked at the port of Lisbon when news arrived of Maximilian's demise. Portugal acquired a cheap statue, quickly adapted it and presented it to the city as Dom Pedro IV.

On the north side of the square stands the **Teatro Nacional de Dona Maria,** built in the 1840s on the site of the Inquisitors' Palace. In the northwest corner, past the neo-Manueline Rossio station is the Praça dos Restauradores, marking the restoration of the Portuguese monarchy in 1640 after 60 years of Spanish occupation.

At the far end of the square catch the clanking funicular, known as the Elevador da Gloria, up to the Bairro Alto. Alternatively head back down through the Rossio and just off Rua do Ouro is the Elevador de Santa Justa. One of Lisbon's landmarks, the 45m (147ft) elevator and viaduct was built in 1901 by Raul Mesnier de Ponsard, a student of Gustav Eiffel, to link the Baixa to the Rua do Carmo above. It offers great views of the whole area.

✚ *Lisboa 3b*

Teatro Nacional de Dona Maria

✉ Praça Dom Pedro IV ☎ 213 250 835 Ⓜ Rossio

Castelo de São Jorge

Crowning a hill surrounded by the Alfama district, the castle is built on 5th-century Visigoth and 9th-century Moorish foundations. The present 12th- to 14th-century edifice was begun by Afonso Henriques, following his capture of Lisbon from the Moors in 1147. A climb up through the Alfama district to the top is rewarded by stupendous views over the Tagus and its suspension bridge, and by beautiful gardens planted when the castle was restored in 1938.

www.castelosaojorge.egeac.pt

🗺 *Lisboa 4b* 🕐 Mar–Oct daily 9–8:30; Nov–Feb daily 9–5:30 ☎ 218 800 620 💷 Moderate 🚌 Bus 37, tram 12, 28

Mosteiro dos Jéronimos

Best places to see, pages 44–45.

Museu Calouste Gulbenkian

Best places to see, pages 46–47.

Museu da Marinha

This is the place to go if you want to understand how, in the 15th and 16th centuries, Portugal rose to become one of the greatest maritime and trading powers on earth. The Maritime Museum houses maps, documents, navigational instruments and models of ships from the era of discoveries through to this century. There is also an interesting section on naval aviation.

www.museu.marinha.pt

➕ *Lisboa 1d (off map)* ✉ Praça do Império ☎ 213 620 019 🕓 May–Sep Tue–Sun 10–6; Oct–Apr Tue–Sun 10–5. Closed public hols 🖐 Inexpensive. Free Sun 10–1 🚌 Buses from the Baixa district, tram 15

Museu Nacional dos Coches

Immediately to the east of the Presidential Palace at Belém, in a former riding school, is the Coach Museum, with its superb collection of horse-drawn coaches. The collection spans three centuries and comes from royal households around Europe including Portugal, Spain, France and Italy.

Some are extravagant and ornate – glittering with gold and lined with velvet. Pride of place goes to a sumptuous trio of coaches built in Rome for the Portuguese ambassador to the Vatican, the better to project an image of Portugal as a proud and wealthy nation.

www.museudoscoches-ipmuseus.pt

🚍 *Lisboa 1d (off map)* ✉ Praça Afonso de Albuquerque, Belém ⏰ Tue–Sun 10–6. Closed public hols ♿ Inexpensive. Free Sun 10–2 🚌 Buses from the Baixa district, tram 15

Oceanário

This spectacular oceanarium in the Parque das Nações (Park of the Nations)

is the largest in Europe. It opened in 1998 as the centrepiece of the Expo '98 world exposition and has become one of Lisbon's most popular visitor attractions. It features a huge central tank (the largest in Europe), with four others around it, representing the world's oceans.

www.oceanario.pt

➕ *Lisboa 6a (off map)* ✉ Esplanada D Carlos 1, Parque dos Nações ☎ 21 891 7002 🕐 Daily 10–7 (until 6 Nov–Mar) 👆 Expensive 🚇 Oriente

Padrão dos Descobrimentos

The huge, triumphalist Monument to the Discoveries was unveiled in 1960 to mark the 500th anniversary of Prince Henry the Navigator's death. Curved to the seaward side and angular on the other, it also represents a ship's prow, and serves as a memorial to all players in the Portuguese Age of Discoveries. A lift (elevator) whisks you to the top, from where there are views over the city: the Tagus estuary spanned by the great 25 de Abril suspension bridge to the west, and the new Vasco da Gama bridge to the east.

www.padraodescobrimentos.egeac.pt

➕ *Lisboa 1d (off map)* ✉ Belém 🕐 May–Sep Tue–Sun 10–6:30; Oct–Apr Tue–Sun 10–5:30 👆 Moderate 🚌 Buses from the Baixa district, tram 15

a walk around Lisbon

Start at the Praça do Comércio.

This is Lisbon's bustling centre, also frequently called by its old name Terreiro do Paço, after the royal palace which stood here until its destruction in the 1755 earthquake. It is set on the river with the Castelo São Jorge towering above.

Follow the long, straight, pedestrianized Rua Augusta away from the river. There is frequently an almost carnival atmosphere along here, with street performers and vendors selling flowers, roasted chestnuts and lottery tickets. The road runs into Rossio Square.

Rossio Square is lined with cafés spilling outside, aflutter with pigeons, and presided over by a statue of the playwright Gil Vincente adorning the façade of the Dona Maria II National Theatre. This is Lisbon at its liveliest; stop a while and watch the world go by.

Leave the square via Rua Áurea at the southwest corner. One block along is the iron-girdered Elevador de Santa Justa. Take this lift up to the top for glorious views over the city. A bridge leads from the lift, onto Rua do Carmo. On the right is the Convento do Carmo.

Wander around the atmospheric ruins of this Carmelite convent, which tumbled down in the 1755 earthquake, and was never rebuilt. It is easy to forget that you are in the middle of the city.

Cross to the other side of the Largo do Carmo, turn left onto Rua Serpa Pinto, and left again into Rua Garrett.

Named after author Almeida Garrett, this is one of Lisbon's most fashionable and interesting streets. On the left, at number 20, is the famous A Brasileira. This gilt and mirrored coffee house, with a bronze statue of poet Fernando Pessoa outside, simply oozes atmosphere. It has long been a haunt of Lisbon's literary circle.

Distance 3.5km (2 miles)
Time About 3 hours
Start point Praça do Comércio ✚ *Lisboa 3c*
End point Rua Garrett ✚ *Lisboa 3b*
Lunch Cervejaria da Trindade (€€) ✉ Rua Nova da Trindade 20-c
(adjacent to Largo do Carmo)

Sé

Like many Portuguese cathedrals, including those at Porto, Évora and the Sé Velha at Coimbra, Lisbon's cathedral was originally a fortress as well as a place of worship. Sturdy twin crenellated towers, rising above the façade, are testimony to this. It was founded in the 12th century following the conquest of the Moors and, from the outside, maintains a distinct Romanesque mien.

The interior tells a fuller story of Portuguese architectural history. The nave is in plain, somewhat austere Romanesque style, but the ambulatory and lancet windows are Gothic. There is a beautiful baroque crib and a fine 17th-century organ.

A side chapel houses the tombs and stone effigies of notables including archbishops of Lisbon and Lopo Fernandes Pacheco, a 14th-century comrade-in-arms of King Afonso IV, with a dog at his feet. Off this chapel are the 13th-century monastic cloisters. A door from the south transept leads into the sacristy, where treasures and religious art are displayed in the Museu do Tesouro da Sé. Try not to miss the mother-of-pearl oriental casket, said to contain relics of St Vincent.

➕ *Lisboa 4c* ✉ Largo da Sé 🕐 Museum daily 10–5; Cloister daily 10–6; Cathedral daily 9–7 💲 Church free; cloisters inexpensive. Free Sun am

Torre de Belém

This 16th-century fortress on the edge of the Tagus has defended the capital and housed political prisoners; today it is one of Lisbon's most photogenic landmarks, looking almost like a tall ship tethered to the quayside and floating serenely on the river. Inside is a museum of weapons and armour, and you can climb to the top of the tower for views over the Tagus estuary.

➕ *Lisboa 1d (off map)* ✉ Avenida de Brasília ☎ 213 620 034 🕐 May–Sep Tue–Sun 10–6:30; Oct–Apr Tue–Sun 10–5 (last entry 30 mins before closing 💲 Moderate 🚌 Tram 15 from Baixa, bus 29, 43 from Belém

More to see in Central Portugal

ALCOBAÇA
Best places to see, pages 36–37.

BATALHA
Best places to see, pages 38–39.

CASCAIS
Cascais is a stylish, large and still-burgeoning holiday resort. It is also a commuter town for wealthy Lisboetas. Echoing the story of so many fishing ports, especially in the Algarve, the centre of activity is now the tourist trade, with scores of hotels and restaurants, but catches are still unloaded daily on the beach and auctioned in the local market.

www.cm-cascais.pt

➕ 7T ✉ 32km (20 miles) west of Lisbon and 13km (8 miles) from Sintra

ℹ Rua Visconde da Luz ☎ 214 868 204

ESTORIL

Portugal's most popular holiday resort north of the Algarve was famous long before the 1960s tourist explosion. Since the end of the 19th century the town has attracted the rich and famous from around Europe, and in the 1940s and 1950s became home to various deposed crowned heads, such as King Humberto of Italy and King Juan Carlos of Spain.

Some imposing façades and the casino recall this era, although the other facilities are as up-to-date as anywhere. This combination of an old-fashioned holiday ambience and the new cosmopolitan image gives Estoril an atmosphere which is the antithesis of quaint. On warm weekends, and particularly during the summer holidays, you'll find the town bustling as wealthy Lisboetas flock to enjoy the beaches and the wealth of excellent restaurants.

www.estorilcoast-tourism.com

🚉 7T ✉ 29km (18 miles) from Lisbon

🛈 Arcadas do Parque ☎ 214 663 813

a drive along the Arrábida Coast

Leave Lisbon via the 2km-long (1.2-mile) 25 de Abril suspension bridge, leaving the IP7 motorway at the second exit and following the N378 to Santana. Turn right here, onto the N379 to Cabo Espichel.

Cabo Espichel is a desolate, wind-fretted cape at the furthest end of a barren plateau. It has a raw beauty to it as you look out over towering, sea-battered cliffs.

Return to Santana, and turn right, twisting down for a couple of kilometres to Sesimbra.

Sesimbra is an attractive fishing port and resort, though its popularity has brought mass tourist development on the surrounding hills.

Return to Santana and take the N397 again heading east. After 8km (5 miles) turn right at signs for Portinho da Arrábida, into the Parque Natural da Arrábida.

The road leads through vineyards and orchards before climbing into the Serra da Arrábida hills.

After 10km (6 miles) the road splits. Signs for Portinho da Arrábida lead right, down to the south coast where there are excellent beaches, but take the left fork and the road travels along the spine of the Serra da Arrábida with outstanding views south to the flat peninsula of the Tróia and the Sado Estuary. Once the road descends, at the T-junction (intersection) turn left (signposted Lisbon and Azietão) to reach the village of Vila Nogueira da Azietão.

This is the headquarters of the Fonseca winery. Here you can visit the cellars and taste the latest wines.

Distance 75km (46 miles)
Time 6 hours including stops
Start point 25 de Abril Bridge ✚ 8T
End point Vila Nogueira da Azietão ✚ 8T
Lunch Nova Fortaleza (€€) ✉ Largo dos Bombaldes, Sesimbra ☎ 212 232 081

FÁTIMA

Fátima is one of the principal places of pilgrimage in the Roman Catholic world. On 13 May 1917 three peasant children saw a vision of the Virgin Mary speaking to them from the top of an oak tree. She warned of cataclysmic events about to take place in Russia, and pleaded for prayer and sacrifice as prerequisites for peace in the world. Further apparitions took place on the 13th day of each subsequent month, culminating in an inexplicable spectacle on 13 October, when 70,000 onlookers saw the sun spinning like a ball in the sky. Many of these witnesses are still alive. Two of the children died soon afterwards, but the third, Sister Lucia, lived as a Carmelite nun until her death in 2006.

The phenomenon sparked a spiritual regeneration in Portugal. Millions visit the site every year, including upwards of 100,000 on 13 May and 13 October. A basilica has been built on the spot of the apparitions with a vast paved area where the faithful gather. There are dozens of cheap hotels and hundreds of stalls selling tacky religious artefacts.

Fátima has nothing for the sceptical. Others find spiritual energy here.

www.santuario-fatima.pt

🚌 1K ✉ 20km (12 miles) east of Batalha

🛈 Avenida José Alves Correia da Silva

☎ 249 531 139

LEIRIA

Leiria is a pleasant little town on the River Liz, clustering around a perpendicular rock topped by a forbidding medieval **castle.** Inside a ring of defensive walls is the sheer keep and the royal palace with its vast hall. At night the castle is floodlit and shines like a beacon for miles around.

www.rt-leiriafatima.pt

➕ 1J ✉ 67km (42 miles) south of Coimbra

ℹ Jardim Luís de Camões ☎ 244 848 770

Castle

🕐 Apr–Sep Tue–Sun 10–6; Oct–Mar Tue–Sun 9:30–5:30 👋 Inexpensive

ÓBIDOS

Best places to see, pages 48–49.

SANTARÉM

The capital of the Ribatejo region is a bustling town on the west bank of the Tagus, which serves as the agricultural hub for the fertile outlying plains. These days Santarém is best known as the bullfighting and dressage capital of Portugal. Fine specimens of bulls and horses can be seen grazing in the rich pastures surrounding the town – horsemanship was developed as a means of fighting the bulls by mounted *cavaleiros*.

However, Santarém is not a place to linger, unless you are there during the last week in October or first week in November (it differs from year to year), when the great National Gastronomic Fair is held, and you can wander from stall to stall tasting regional titbits from all over Portugal, amid fireworks and jollity.

www.cm-santarem.pt

➕ 9R ✉ 78km (48 miles) northeast of Lisbon

ℹ 63 Rua de Capelo Ivens ☎ 243 304 200

SINTRA

High on a hilltop and surrounded by dense, green forests, Sintra has inspired poets as diverse as Camões and Byron, during centuries of its popularity among writers, artists, musicians and European high society. The town was a summer retreat for royalty

up until the abolition of the monarchy in 1910. A leisurely saunter along the forest trails is highly recommended before any sightseeing.

So many different Portuguese monarchs added their own embellishments to the **Palácio Nacional** that the whole defies any architectural classification. The two wings added by Manuel II in the 16th century sit awkwardly with the main structure.

Inside, the palace tour takes you through an astonishing diversity of rooms – each one a folly of one king or another. In the Magpie Room are 136 magpies, each with a rose in its beak representing the ladies of the court, one of whom King João is said to have presented with a rose when Queen Philippa wasn't looking. A magpie stole the rose, drawing the Queen's attention to her husband's philandering, so the story goes.

In the hills of the Serra de Sintra that surround the town is the 8th-century Castelo dos Mouros with commanding views over Sintra and the National Palace, and the Palácio Nacional da Pena, built in the mid-18th century by Ferdinand, husband of Queen Maria II. The pastel coloured riot of towers, turrets and arches is truly neo-Gothic in style and holds a wealth of period furniture including vast tapestries.

www.cm-sintra.pt

✚ 7S ✉ 28km (17 miles) northwest of Lisbon

🛈 Praça da República ☎ 21 923 1157

Palácio Nacional

✉ Largo Rainha Dona Amália ☎ 219 106 840 🕒 Thu–Tue 10–5:30 (last admission 5). Closed public hols. Tours every 20 mins ✋ Moderate

TOMAR

Tomar is the architectural jewel of the Ribatejo region and should not be missed by anybody with an interest in historic buildings. It is also a pleasant little town on the banks of the River Nabão with some good hotels and restaurants, making it an excellent place for visitors to stop for the night.

The immense, fortified, hilltop **Convento de Cristo** (Convent of Christ) dominates Tomar. Parts of the crenellated walls date from the 12th century, when it was a stronghold of the Knights Templar, the powerful military order founded to keep pilgrim routes open to the Holy Land during the Crusades, and answerable only to the Pope. After it was disbanded by Pope Clement V in 1330, King Dinis created in its place the Order of the Knights of Christ, with its seat at Tomar.

🔁 2K ✉ 135km (84 miles) northeast of Lisbon

ℹ Avenida Dr Cândido Madureira

☎ 249 322 427

Convento de Cristo

🕐 Jun–Sep daily 9–6; Oct–May daily 9–5

✋ Moderate ❓ Tomar's *Festa dos Tabuleiros* (Festival of the Trays), one of Portugal's most famous festivals, takes place every four years on 2nd Sun in Jul (dates vary; next in 2011)

HOTELS

ALCOBAÇA
Hotel Santa Maria (€)
This modest, friendly hotel is the best of a very limited choice of lodgings in town.
✉ Rua Dr Franciso Zagalo 20–22 ☎ 262 597 395

BATALHA
Residencial Casa do Outeiro (€)
This modern small pension makes a good budget option. All rooms have terraces, some with views of the monastery. Small pool.
✉ Largo Carvalho do Outeiro 4 ☎ 244 765 806; www.casadoouteiro.com

CASCAIS
Hotel Albatroz (€€€)
A superb, if very pricey, luxury hotel in a converted palace. The old rooms have more character but a new wing offers greater comfort.
✉ Rua Federico Arouca 100 ☎ 214 847 380; www.albatrozhotels.com

ESTORIL
São Cristovão (€)
Beautiful, very small seafront *pensão* that has managed to retain its character.
✉ Avenida Marginal 7079 ☎ 214 680 913

FÁTIMA
Estalagem Dom Gonçalo (€€)
Refurbished modern hotel set in woodland. A popular spot with pilgrims. Run by Best Western.
✉ Rua Jacinta Marto 100 ☎ 249 539 330; www. estalgemdomgoncalo.com

LISBON
As Janelas Verdes (€€€)
Restored 18th-century mansion house in the Lapa district. There is a small garden with a terrace where you can relax.
✉ Rua das Janelas Verdes 47 ☎ 213 968 143; www.heritage.pt

Avenida Palace (€€€)
Classical, old-style opulence and superlative service.
✉ Rua 1 Dezembro 123 ☎ 213 218 100; www.hotel-avenida-palace.pt

Roma (€)
Pleasant little *pensão*, near the Avenida da Liberdade.
✉ Travessa da Gloria 22a ☎ 213 460 557; www.residencialroma-lisbon.com

Solar do Castelo (€€€)
A medieval structure close to Castelo São Jorge tastefully
converted into a stylish hotel.
✉ Rua das Cozinhas 2 ☎ 218 806 050; www.heritage.pt

York House (€€€)
Converted monastery offering the atmosphere of a country *quinta*.
✉ Rua das Janelas Verdes 32 ☎ 213 962 435; www.yorkhouselisboa.com

ÓBIDOS
Albergaria Rainha Santa Isabel (€–€€)
A modest friendly place with rooms with balconies overlooking a
narrow street.
✉ Rua Direita ☎ 262 959 323; www.arsio.com

Pousada do Castelo (€€€)
Portugal's smallest *pousada*, and one of the most romantic places
in the country to stay.
☎ 262 955 080; www.pousadas.pt

PALMELA
Pousada de Palmela (€€€)
Glorious *pousada* within superb views over the Arrábida peninsula.
✉ Castelo de Palmela 2950–3A, Palmela ☎ 212 351 226; www.pousadas.pt

QUELUZ
Pousada da Dona Maria I (€€€)
Wonderful *pousada*; convenient for the Peninsular War battle sites.
✉ Largo Palácio de Queluz ☎ 214 356 158; www.pousadas.pt

SINTRA
Hotel Tivoli Palácio de Seteais (€€–€€€)
A converted 18th-century palace set in spectacular gardens.

✉ Rua Barbosa du Bocage 8–10 ☎ 219 233 200; www.tivolihotels.com

TOMAR
Estalagem Santa Iria (€€)
Enchanting little inn on an island. Convenient for the town sites.

✉ Parque do Mouchão ☎ 249 313 326; www.estalagemiria.com

RESTAURANTS

ALCOBAÇA
Trindade (€€)
An excellent place to dine, right by the abbey.

✉ Praça Dom Henriques 22 ☎ 262 582 397 ⏰ Closed Sat

BATALHA
Estalagem Mestre Afonso Domingues (€€)
Right next to the monastery, serving a fine meal, preceded by delicious cured ham and cheesy titbits.

☎ 244 765 260

CASCAIS
Jardim dos Frangos (€)
Grilled chicken and sardines with fresh salad. Expect to queue.

✉ Avenida dos Combatentes da Grande Guerra 168 ☎ 214 861 717

O Pescador (€€)
Excellent choice of fresh seafood but the paella is a speciality.

✉ Rua das Flores 10B ☎ 214 832 054

LEIRIA
Tromba Rija (€€)
The fixed menu features fantastic starters, main courses, regional desserts and wine.

✉ Rua Professor Portelas 22 ☎ 244 852 277 ⏰ Fri–Sat lunch and dinner, Sun lunch only

LISBON

Belcanto (€€)

Formal restaurant serving classic Portuguese cuisine including locally renowned *Ovos à Professor*, an egg dish.

✉ Largo de São Carlos 10 ☎ 213 420 607 🕔 Closed Sat and Sun

Bota Alta (€€)

A small, simple restaurant at the heart of the Bairro Alto serving good, hearty food.

✉ Travessa da Queimada 35–37 ☎ 213 427 959 🕔 Closed Sat lunch and Sun

Forno Velho (€€)

A first rate Brazilian restaurant serving large plates of barbecued meats and *feijoada* (bean stew).

✉ Rua do Salitre 42 ☎ 213 533 706 🕔 Closed Sun lunch

Gambrinus (€€€)

Best place in the Baixa district for seafood and fresh fish.

✉ Rua Portas de Santo Antão 23 ☎ 213 421 466

Sua Exelencia (€€€)

Romantic little restaurant in the Lapa district, where the owner often introduces himself personally to the guests.

✉ Rua do Conde 34 ☎ 213 903 614 🕔 Closed Wed

Tágide (€€€)

One of Lisbon's top restaurants, located on fashionable Rua Garrett. High class international cuisine.

✉ Largo da Academia Nacional de Belas Artes 18 ☎ 213 420 720 🕔 Closed Sat and Sun

ÓBIDOS

A llustre Casa de Ramiro (€€)

Regional cuisine served in an atmospheric dining room of stone and deep pastel pink stucco – a magnet for the 'smart set'.

✉ Rua Porto do Vale ☎ 262 959 194 🕔 Closed Thu

Muralhas (€€)

Fashionable and arty visitors to Óbidos come here for high quality, traditional Portuguese cooking.

✉ Rua Dom João de Ornelas ☎ 262 959 930

Pousada do Castelo (€€)

A richly atmospheric and romantic place in which to dine. It's also very popular, so reserving a table is highly recommended.

✉ Castelo de Óbidos ☎ 262 955 080

SANTARÉM
O Mal Cozinhado (€)

Excellent value food served in this restaurant, located in the town which holds a well-regarded annual gastronomic fair.

✉ Campo Emílio Infante da Câmara ☎ 243 323 584

SETÚBAL
Pousada de São Filipe (€€)

The magnificent views from the terrace atop the fortress walls match the food served at this most dramatic *pousada*.

✉ Fortress São Filipe ☎ 265 550 070

SINTRA
Tacho Real (€€)

This restaurant serves a selection of excellent food, both Portuguese and international, at reasonable prices.

✉ Rua da Ferreira 4 ☎ 21 923 5277 ⊘ Closed Mon

SHOPPING

GLASS, PORCELAIN AND CERAMICS
Atlantis

A full range of Atlantis crystal.

✉ Amoreiras Shopping Centre, Avenida Duarte Pacheco, Lisbon

Cerâmicas de São Pedro

Hand-crafted *azulejos* panels. Shipping can be arranged.

✉ Calçada de São Pedro 32, Sintra ☎ 219 243 306

Fábrica Ceramica Viúva Lamego
Hand-painted tiles straight from this factory that also has a shop. Some good deals on seconds.
✉ Largo do Intendente 25, Lisbon ☎ 218 852 408

Jasmin
Hand-made high quality glass items are sold in the factory shop.
✉ Estrada de Leiria 227, Marinha Grande ☎ 244 575 590

HANDICRAFTS AND SOUVENIRS
A Artesã
Portuguese linen and cotton tablecloths, napkins etc, from mass produced to expensive hand woven and embroidered.
✉ Rua Direita 91, Óbidos ☎ 262 959 392

Alfazema
It's hard to choose just one item from Alfazema's excellent range of fine linens and embroidery.
✉ Largo 1 de Dezembro 10, São Pedro de Sintra ☎ 219 231 131

Centro de Turismo e Artesanato
A wide range of ceramics, glass, leather and other handicrafts, from all over Portugal. Packing and shipment can be arranged.
✉ Rua Castilho 61B, Lisbon ☎ 213 863 830

JEWELLERY
W A Sarmento
One of Lisbon's longest established goldsmiths, with a beautiful selection of jewellery. Also does individual commission.
✉ Rua do Ouro (da Aurea) 251, Lisbon ☎ 213 426 779

MARKET
Lisbon Flea Market
The capital's largest outdoor market for handicrafts, clothes, food, rugs and much more. Behind São Vincente church.
✉ Campo de Santa Clara ◷ Tue, Sat

WINE
Solar do Vinho do Porto
The place to buy port in the capital.
✉ Rua São Pedro de Alcântara 45, Lisbon ☎ 213 475 707

ENTERTAINMENT

CASINO
Casino Estoril
✉ Estoril ☎ 214 667 700; www.casino-estoril.pt

DISCOS AND NIGHTCLUBS
Kapital
Ultra-trendy, somewhat cliquey. Mainly techno music downstairs, more middle-of-the-road on the other two floors.
✉ Avenida 24 de Junho 68, Lisbon

Kremlin
One of the city's long-standing late-night venues attracting the fashionable young things.
✉ Escadinhas da Praia 5, Lisbon

Lux–Frágil
A long-established but still very popular nightclub set on the banks of the river.
✉ Avenida Infante D Henrique, Armazém A, Cais da Pedra Santa Apolónia, Lisbon

Nuts Club
The hottest disco on the Lisbon coast, full of energetic Lisboetas and foreign tourists.
✉ Avenida Rei Humberto II de Itália 7, Cascais

Plateau
Long established nightclub that still has many devotees.
✉ Escadinhas da Praia 3–7, Lisbon

FADO
Adega Mesquita

A popular venue with locals and tourists.

✉ Rua Diário da Notícias, Lisbon ☎ 213 219 280

A Severa

One of Lisbon's best known clubs, where top fadistas perform.

✉ Rua das Gáveas 55, Lisbon ☎ 213 428 314

Clube de Fado

A chic modern interior for this *fado* club.

✉ Rua São João de Praça, Lisbon ☎ 218 852 704

Senhor Vinho

Top-notch, genuine *fado* performances, at reasonable prices.

✉ Rua do Meio à Lapa 18, Lisbon ☎ 213 972 681 ◷ Closed Sun

Timpanas

Well away from the city centre, but this venue is well worth seeking out if you are eager to listen to the real McCoy.

✉ Rua Gilberto Rola 24, Alcântara, Lisbon ☎ 213 906 655 ◷ Closed Wed

THEATRE
Teatro Municipal de São Luiz

Another grand, old-fashioned theatre where Portuguese and international companies perform.

✉ Rua António Maria Cardoso 40, Lisbon ☎ 213 257 640

Teatro Nacional de Dona Maria II

Lisbon's principal theatre holds performances of Portuguese and foreign plays throughout the year except summer. All productions are in Portuguese.

✉ Praça Dom Pedro IV, Lisbon ☎ 213 250 835; www.teatro-dmaria.pt

Teatro National de São Carlos

Stages opera and ballet productions and classical music concerts.

✉ Largo São Carlos, Lisbon ☎ 213 253 045

Évora and the Alentejo

Alentejo means, literally, 'beyond the Tagus' and is a great, sun-baked plain bordered to the east by a backbone of high craggy mountains and the wide Guadiana river, which together form a natural border with Spain. The glorious, historic towns have a sleepy feel to them which defies the pivotal roles they have all played in Portuguese history.

Évora

The region covers over a third of the total area of Portugal but is home to barely a tenth of the population, so the Alentejo has a slow, little-changing pace of life.

Other than a scattering of superb *pousadas*, such as the converted national monuments in Évora and Estremoz, accommodation of a high standard is fairly scarce, although there are growing numbers of very comfortable bed-and-breakfast-style places. For as long as this remains the case, the Alentejo can be expected to maintain its remote, arcane atmosphere and its treasures will remain undiscovered by mass tourism.

ÉVORA

Évora crowns a gentle hill, rising from the sunbaked plains of the Alentejo, surrounded by expansive fields of wheat, olive groves and cork forest. Almost entirely enclosed within sturdy, 14th-century walls, it is the sort of place a sightseer's dreams are made of, and one of the great joys of travelling in Portugal.

Évora is almost a museum of Portuguese art and architecture in itself. So extensive is the collection of historic buildings, packed tightly together within massive, stone city walls, that in 1986 UNESCO declared Évora a World Heritage Site.

Fittingly, one of the city's finest architectural treasures, the 15th-century Convento dos Lóios, can be enjoyed to the full by guests of the hotel, but not the general public. It has been imaginatively converted into a *pousada*, with guests staying in the old monastic cells and eating (meditatively or otherwise) in the dining room along two sides of the main cloister quadrangle. After dinner you can relax in the chapter house, now the lounge.

The many other points of interest can all be easily explored on foot, as you wander along cobbled streets lined with cafés, enlivened by the city's sizeable student population. By night, floodlights bathe the city in luminous green, making it look from afar like a giant glow-worm; this makes Évora a romantic place for an after-dinner stroll.

www.cm-evora.pt/guiaturistico

🚌 10T

ℹ️ Praça do Giraldo ☎ 266 730 030

Igreja de São Francisco

Think carefully about whether you really want to see the Church of St Francis. Thousands of people do every year, on account of the famous Capela dos Ossos (Chapel of Bones); many leave revolted. The chapel, built by a macabre monk in the 15th century, is decorated with designs made from the bones of 5,000 human skeletons. There are skulls grinning at you from every direction, while at the far end of the chapel hang the shrivelled, leathery corpses of a man and a child. The smell of death seems to linger in the air, while an inscription in Portuguese translates menacingly as: 'We the bones lie in wait for yours'.

You reach the chapel through a chapterhouse where wax images of parts of the human body have been placed as votive offerings, by faithful pilgrims with ailments (the voluminous wax breasts are the petitions of infertile women). The braids of hair pinned to the wall at the chapel entrance are cut from brides, as an offering before their wedding.

Escape into the open air can be a welcome relief after this piece of sightseeing.

✚ *Évora 2c* ✉ Praça 1° de Maio ☎ 266 709 521 🕐 Daily 9–12:30, 2:30–5:15 💰 Main church free; Chapel of Bones inexpensive

a walk around Évora

Start outside the Convento dos Lóios (➤ 144) on the Largo Marquês de Marialva square, at the centre of which is the city's Roman temple (➤ 150).

The remains of this temple, built between the first and third century AD, constitute the most outstanding Roman monument in Portugal. Parts of it have been dismantled for other building works over the centuries, but 12 of the Corinthian-style columns on marble plinths are perfectly intact. It is particularly beautiful floodlit at night.

Before leaving the square, also check out the cathedral (➤ 148–149). Walk under an arch behind the cathedral apse, and turn left to follow down a narrow street to the Antiga Universidade (Old University).

Walk around the cool, two-storey cloister and admire the fine *azulejo* tiles in the lecture rooms.

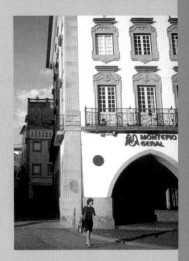

Walk down narrow Rua Conde da Serra da Tourega, turning left into Largo das Portas de Moura, where there is a fine, Manueline stone fountain, shaped as a globe. Notice the splendidly ornate façade of Casa Cordovil. Walk back across the square to the Igreja da Misericórdia.

Misericórdia is worth seeing for the fine baroque altar, and *azulejo*-embellished walls.

Return to Largo das Portas de Moura, this time turning right onto Rua Miguel Bombarda and left onto Rua da República, down to Igreja São Francisco (▶ 145). Walk back up Rua da República, and left up the hill into Praça do Giraldo.

Évora's main square, Praça do Giraldo, is cobbled with black and white stones, and arcaded round the sides, leaving open-air cafés coolly shaded.

Distance 2km (1.2 miles)
Time 3–4 hours
Start point Largo Marquês de Marialva ✚ *Évora 3b*
End point Praça do Giraldo ✚ *Évora 2b*
Lunch Café Arcada (€) ✉ Praça do Giraldo ☎ 266 741 777

Sé

Cross to the opposite side of the Largo da Sé, beyond the Roman temple (➤ 150), to appreciate the full glory of Évora's fortress-like cathedral, with its 12th- and 13th-century façade and the two huge, dissimilar towers built 400 years later. On the way in, look for the carved stone statues of the 12 apostles guarding the entrance, probably the work of French and Portuguese sculptors between 1322 and 1340. In the soaring nave, with its barrel vaulting and beautiful transept dome, vast chandeliers hang from the ceiling. Don't miss the rose windows – the north one shows the Morning Star and the south the Mystic Rose. The oak choir stalls contain fine decorated panels.

A staircase at the back leads to the cathedral's fascinating Museu de Arte Sacra (Museum of Sacred Art), which houses a glittering collection of treasures including crucifixes and offertory chalices in gold and silver studded with diamonds and emeralds, the vestments and mitres of full episcopal pomp and ceremony and – by far the most beautiful exhibit in the museum – a 13th-century carved ivory statue of the Virgin of Paradise.

The 14th-century Gothic cloisters are reached through a door in the cathedral nave. Climb any of the corner staircases up onto the battlements for wonderful views over the town, and the plains of the Alentejo beyond.

🕂 *Évora 3b* ✉ Largo da Sé ☎ 266 759 330 🕙 Church: Jun–Sep daily 9–5; Oct–May daily 9–12:15, 2–4:45. Museum: Jun–Sep daily 9–5; Oct–May daily 9–12, 2–4:30 💵 Church inexpensive; church and cloister inexpensive; church, cloister and museum moderate

Templo Romano

Set on the hill to the west of the Sé, this ruin is Portugal's best preserved Roman structure and Évora's most distinguished landmark. There is some question as to when it was built, though most agree it was between the first and third centuries. Although it is known locally as the Templo de Diana, it is believed to have been constructed as a shrine to the cult of the Emperor Augustus. Set on a 3m (10ft) granite base, 14 of its original 18 Corinthian columns still remain standing as well as most of the architrave and detailed capitals. Columns, bases and capitals are all crafted from white marble from nearby Estremoz.

The Middle Ages saw it serve as a fortress and later as a slaughterhouse, a function which almost certainly saved it from demolition.

✝ *Évora 3b* ✋ Free

More to see in the Alentejo

BEJA

Reputedly the hottest place in Portugal, but a pleasant town with several points of historical interest. The 15th-century Convento da Nossa Senhora de Conceição, home to the **Museu Regional,** is one of the most beautiful buildings in the Alentejo. It was here that the convent's most famous resident, Sister Mariana Alcoforado, had a love affair with a French count in the 17th century. Her letters were later published as *Letters of a Portuguese Nun.*

➕ 11V 🗺 60km (37 miles) south of Évora
ℹ Rua Capitão João Francisco de Sousa 25 ☎ 284 311 913

Museum

✉ Largo Nossa Senhora de Conceição
🕐 Tue–Sun 9:30–1, 2–5:30
✋ Inexpensive

ELVAS

Elvas stands on the border with Spain and its character has always been shaped by its strategic position. The formidable old town sits within great sturdy ramparts – entrance can only be gained by passing through the old stone gateways. The walls are far more than a gesture of defiance: during the 17th century the ramparts withstood years of repeated and sustained assault and sieges. During the Peninsular War in 1801 Elvas again withstood Spanish attacks and it was despite, rather than because of this that Portugal was forced to capitulate to Spain after the Spanish declared war over Portugal's refusal to break the ancient Anglo-Portuguese alliance. Ten years later, it was from Elvas that Wellington launched his siege of Badajos.

The old quarter is very much lived-in, evident from the sheets flapping from washing lines slung between buildings, from the children who make the ancient squares their playground, and from the hooting of a delivery van as it tries to negotiate an alleyway built long ago for pedestrians and donkeys. Prior to the opening of the A6 motorway, Elvas thrived from the traffic flowing between the two Iberian capitals, providing cheap eateries and lodgings close to the main N4 road.

www.cm-elvas.pt

➕ 12S ✉ 42km (26 miles) east of Estremoz and 10km (6 miles) from the Spanish border

ℹ Tourist Office: Praça da República next to the main bus stop

☎ 268 622 236

ESTREMOZ

Ancient, fortified Estremoz, rising out of the Alentejo flatness, has a medieval atmosphere, felt particularly by

those who stay in the 13th-century royal castle which dominates the town, and which has been turned into a most extraordinary *pousada*.

But just as important a part of Estremoz's fascination is to be discovered as you wander along the historic streets, many of them cobbled, between Moorish squares and past imposing façades. Rising above the royal palace section of the castle is the greyish marble Torre das Três Coroas (Tower of the Three Crowns), so-called because kings Sancho II, Afonso III and Dinis all contributed to its construction. The climb up a steep, worn staircase to the top of the keep is rewarded by a 360-degree panorama as far as Évora, and across to Spain in the east, if the weather is clear.

Within the keep is the beautiful **Capela Rainha Santa Isabel,** adorned with *azulejo* tile paintings recounting the life of this 14th-century queen and saint who dedicated her life to the poor, often in defiance of her husband King Dinis. She died in the town in 1336.

The castle is always open and the key to the chapel can be obtained from the small museum inside the castle.

www.cm-estremoz.pt

🕂 11S ✉ 44km (27 miles) northeast of Évora
ℹ Praça da República 26 ☎ 268 339 200
Capela Rainha Santa Isabel
♿ Free

a drive around eastern Alentejo

A scenically spectacular alternative to the busy main roads between Évora and the Algarve is to take the remote, back roads near the Spanish border.

Turn off the main IP2 at Beja, taking the 260 eastwards to Serpa.

Serpa is a fine place to stop and feel the soul of the Alentejo. The old quarter is dwarfed by the rambling ruins of a fortress and old city walls. But the real joy of the town is to wander the ancient streets lined with whitewashed houses, which more than anywhere evoke the spirit of the Moors.

Take the 260 road eastwards out of town. After just 2.5km (1.5 miles), pull over at the Capela São Gens.

This simple chapel, with its plain columns inside, is believed to be one of only two original Moorish mosques surviving intact

in Portugal. It is worth enjoying the hushed atmosphere of its cool interior for a few moments. Then, if it is lunchtime, try the Estalagem São Gens for good Alentejo cuisine.

Continue on the 260, then bear right on to the 265, crossing the open plains towards the ridge of mountains to the east. The country becomes increasingly wild and remote-feeling, as the road becomes twistier, and you approach Mértola.

Spectacularly perched on a narrow gorge, Mértola is at the River Guadiana's highest navigable point. Curiously, in the village is Portugal's other mosque – now the Igreja Matriz.

Meander on down the Guadiana valley on the 122 road, until you cross into the Algarve shortly past the village of Espîrito Santo, and head for the resorts of the south coast.

Distance 260km (160 miles)
Time 5–8 hours, depending on stops
Start point Évora ✚ 10T
End point Faro, Algarve ✚ 10Y
Lunch Estalagem São Gens (€€€) (just outside Serpa, on the 260 road)
☎ 284 540 420

MARVÃO

This remote medieval town, perched high on a peak of the São Mamede ridge, which forms a natural border with Spain, has inspired poets such as José Amaro, who wrote of Marvão that 'You have Portugal at your feet and, in opening your arms, Spain'. For centuries its location, encased by sheer cliffs, was the reason for its existence and survival as it was virtually unassailable.

A winding road leads up to the craggy summit, where a *pousada* has been built among the handful of tightly clustered houses within the walls, which visitors can walk around for stupendous views over to Spain.

www.cm-marvao.pt

🕂 12R ✉ 24km (15 miles) north of Portalegre

ℹ Largo de Santa Maria ☎ 245 909 131

MONSARAZ

Best places to see, pages 42–43.

VILA VIÇOSA

This royal city was once the seat of the Dukes of Braganza, the family which provided Portugal with its monarchs from 1640 until the proclamation of the Republic in 1910. It is worth stopping at, to visit the **Paço Ducal** (Ducal Palace), whose 110m-long (360ft) marble façade forms one side of the main square.

The palace is now a museum, filled with huge paintings depicting Portugal's military triumphs – particularly those over the Spanish – along with displays of fine art, porcelain, tapestries and other treasures from the royal era. Also worth seeing are a collection of royal carriages and the kitchens, where enormous, gleaming copper cauldrons and huge roasting spits evoke the era of royal hunting and feasting.

✚ 12T ⊠ 18km (11 miles) southeast of Estremoz

ℹ Praça da República ☎ 268 881 101

Paço Ducal

☎ 268 980 659 ◉ Apr–Sep daily Tue 2–5, Wed–Fri 10–1, 2:30–5:30, Sat–Sun 9:30–1, 2:30–6; Oct–Mar Tue 2–5, Wed 10–1, 2–5, Thu 10–1, 2–5:30, Fri–Sun 9:30–1, 2–5. Closed public hols ✋ Moderate

HOTELS

BEJA

Pousada de São Francisco (€€€)

Splendidly converted, 13th-century Franciscan monastery in the heart of the old town. Rooms are stylishly furnished and many look out over the swimming pool and palm-filled gardens.

✉ Largo Nuno Alvares Pereira ☎ 284 328 441; www.pousadas.pt

Residencial Bejense (€)

This prettily decorated town house in the centre of town is an excellent budget option.

✉ Rua Capitão Francisco de Sousa 57 ☎ 284 311 570

Residencial Santa Barbara (€)

Simple but spotlessly clean and modern, with a great central location.

✉ Rua de Mértola 56 ☎ 284 312 280; www.residencialsantabarbara.pt

CRATO

Pousada Flor da Rosa (€€€)

A 14th-century Templar castle, convent and palace are brought together with an ultra-modern extension to create a picturesque *pousada*. The restaurant serves local cuisine.

✉ 7430–999 Crato ☎ 245 997210; www.pousadas.pt

ELVAS

Pousada de Santa Luzia (€€–€€€)

A comfortable, modern *pousada* outside the walls. Good restaurant serving traditional local specialities.

✉ Avenida de Badajoz ☎ 268 637 470; www.pousadas.pt

Quinta de Santo António (€–€€)

Exquisite old inn, luxuriously restored.

✉ São Bras ☎ 268 636 460; www.quintastoantonio.com

ESTREMOZ
Páteo dos Solares (€€€)
Historic *quinta* (villa) now transformed into a luxury hotel. Some rooms have a fireplace or Jacuzzi.

✉ Rua Brito Capelo ☎ 268 338 400; www.pateosolares.com

Pousada da Rainha Santa Isabel (€€€)
A touch austere perhaps, but this is the closest most people in the modern world get to the atmosphere of a medieval castle.

✉ Largo Dom Diniz ☎ 268 332 075; www.pousadas.pt

ÉVORA
Pousada dos Lóios (€€€)
Another atmospheric *pousada* where you can sleep in the 15th-century monastic cells and dine in the cloisters.

✉ Largo do Conde de Vila Flor ☎ 266 730 070; www.pousadas.pt

Residencial Diana (€)
This small cosy hotel in the heart of the town is within a couple of minutes walk from the Cathedral and Praça do Giraldo.

✉ Rua Diogo Cão 2–3 ☎ 266 702 008

MARVÃO
Pousada de Santa Maria (€€–€€€)
Quite simply one of the most sensationally located *pousadas* in Portugal, but well worth the price. Built within a group of medieval village houses.

✉ Rua 24 de Janeiro ☎ 245 993201; www.pousadas.pt

VILA VIÇOSA
Pousada D João IV (€€€)
This former convent makes the ideal luxurious base for touring the eastern Alentejo.

✉ 7160-251 Vila Viçosa ☎ 268 980 742; www.pousadas.pt

RESTAURANTS

BEJA

Alentejano (€€)

Real, as opposed to designer-tourist Alentejo food is served here. Popular with locals for its brimming bowls of soup and big hunks of pork.

✉ Largo dos Duques de Beja 6–7 ☎ 284 323 849 🕓 Closed Fri

Churrasqueira o Alemão (€)

Good choice of barbecued meats at this better than average *churrasqueira*.

✉ Largo dos Duques de Beja ☎ 284 311 490 🕓 Apr–Oct daily; Nov–Mar Tue–Sat pm only

CASTELO DE VIDE

Marino's (€)

Lovely dining room overlooking the Serra de São Mamede, decorated with the owner's collection of eclectic art. Though there is a strong Italian influence, there are also regional dishes on the menu.

✉ Praça Dom Pedro V 6 ☎ 245 901 408

ELVAS

A Bolota Castanha (€€€)

Acclaimed by the national press as one of the best restaurants in the region with its fine tableware and sophisticated menu. Main courses include wild boar with chestnut purée or duck stuffed with raspberries.

✉ Quinta das Janelas Verdes, Terrugem ☎ 268 657 401 🕓 Closed Sun pm and Mon

Centro Artistica Elvense (€)

An excellent place for a quick, tasty snack or the more substantial dish of the day. Next to the bus station.

✉ Praça da República ☎ 268 622 711

Taberna do Adro (€€)

Choose from substantial regional dishes or simply stick with a selection of the fantastic *petiscos (tapas)* available.

✉ Largo João Dias de Deus 1 ☎ 268 661 194 🕐 Closed Wed

ESTREMOZ
Aguias d'Ouro (€€)

Wholesome, homey local fare at reasonable prices.

✉ Rossio do Marquês de pombal 27-1° ☎ 268 333 326

Pousada da Rainha Santa Isabel (€€)

High class Alentejan food with superb views from the dining room at one of Portugal's finest *pousadas*.

✉ Largo Dom Dinis ☎ 268 332 075; www.pousadas.pt

São Rosas (€€€)

Cosy restaurant in the main square of Estremoz citadel serving typical Portuguese cuisine. It gets busy on weekends so it's best to make a reservation.

✉ Largo Dom Dinis 11 ☎ 268 333 345 🕐 Closed Mon

ÉVORA
A Muralha (€)

Good café serving excellent *pasteis de carne* (meat pastries) and other snacks, as well as a cooked dish of the day.

✉ Rua 5 de Outubro 21 ☎ 266 702 284 🕐 Closed Sun

Café Arcada (€)

Large art deco café on the main square in town where you can enjoy Portuguese patisserie and coffee with the locals.

✉ Praça Giraldo ☎ 266 741 777

Cozinha de Santo Humberto (€€€)

The finest food you'll find in Évora. Very attentive service and excellent wine list. It's certainly expensive, but well worth it.

✉ Rua da Moeda 39 ☎ 266 704 251 🕐 Closed Thu

Luar de Janeiro (€€)

A small, cosy restaurant with a formal touch.

✉ Travessa de Janeiro 13 ☎ 266 749 114 🕔 Closed Thu

Martinho (€€)

Trendy restaurant with arty flourishes, serving original interpretations of traditional Alentejo dishes.

✉ Largo Luis de Camões 24 ☎ 266 703 057 🕔 Closed Thu

O Antão (€€)

Modern restaurant which also exhibits the work of local artists.

✉ Rua João de Deus 5–7 ☎ 266 726 459

O Moinho (€€)

Just out of the centre, near the Campo do Juventude, this rustic, converted windmill serves regional food and great soups cooked in an earthenware pot over the open fire. The wine list is stunning.

✉ Rua de Santo André 2-A, Bairro Nossa Senhora do Carmo ☎ 266 771 060

Pousada dos Lóios (€€)

An unforgettable experience: eating in the cloisters of this fabulous, converted 15th-century monastery.

✉ Largo Conde de Vila Flor ☎ 266 730 070; www.pousadas.pt

Restaurante Típico Guiao (€€)

Very popular restaurant whose *ementa Turistica* is good value.

✉ Rua da República 81 ☎ 266 703 071 🕔 Closed Sun pm and Mon

MARVÃO

Pousada de Santa Maria (€€)

This is by far the best place to eat in Marvão, if only for the quite stupendous panorama out across the olive groves and cork trees of the Alentejo plains. The regional food is excellent, especially the local cheeses.

✉ Rua 24 de Janeiro 7 ☎ 245 993 201; www.pousadas.pt

MONSARAZ
Solar de Monsaraz (€€)
Expect a warm welcome in this friendly, family-run eatery. The food is unsophisticated, but very filling.

✉ Rua Conde de Monsaraz 38, Reguengos de Monsaraz ☎ 266 502 846

SERPA
Alentejano (€)
Specialities at this restaurant include rich, meaty dishes and several excellent local ewe's milk cheeses, all at reasonable prices.

✉ Praça da República 8 ☎ 284 544 335 🕐 Closed Mon

Cuiça-Filho (€)
Cheap, cheerful and very friendly, family-run restaurant serving good food.

✉ Rua Portas de Beja 18 ☎ 284 549 566 🕐 Closed Sun

VILA VIÇOSA
Framar (€)
Simple restaurant run by a friendly family. Large portions at very reasonable prices.

✉ Praça da República 35 ☎ 268 980 158 🕐 Closed Mon

Ouro Branco (€€)
A good selection of traditional and distinctive Alentejo dishes is on the menu at this restaurant, including excellent soup.

✉ Campo da Restauração ☎ 268 980 276 🕐 Closed Mon

Pousada D João IV (€€)
Quality regional food in the dining room of this former convent. In summer you can dine outside on the terrace.

✉ 7160 Vila Viçosa ☎ 268 980 742; www.pousadas.pt

SHOPPING

HANDICRAFTS AND SOUVENIRS
Artesanato Diana
One of many handicraft shops along this arterial street, east of Praça do Giraldo. Leather, cork and sheepskin items are sold, along with Alentejan *capotes* – heavy woollen capes with fur collars.
✉ Rua 5 de Outubro 48, Évora ☎ 266 704 609

Coisas do Monte
Excellent collection of woven woollen shawls, scarves and blankets, plus other local handicrafts.
✉ Rua de de São Manços 16, Évora ☎ 266 701 936

Tourist Office
Local handicrafts, pottery and embroidery at reasonable prices.
✉ Largo D João de Melo 2/3, Serpa ☎ 284 544 727

JEWELLERY
Miranda Ferrão
Local gold and silver work including examples of filigree work.
✉ Rua 5 Outubro 28–9, Évora ☎ 266 702 209

MARKETS
Estremoz
Noted for its crafts, pottery and local cheeses.
✉ Rossio do Marquês de Pombal, Estremoz 🕐 Sat 8–1

Évora
Main market in town.
✉ Rossio da São Brás, Évora 🕐 Second Tue of each month

ENTERTAINMENT

DISCO
Oficín@bar
Off the main square in Elvas, friendly bar playing mix of music for all ages.
✉ Rua da Moeda 27, Elvas

Faro and the Algarve

When Portuguese from elsewhere in the country say *Algarve não é Portugal* – 'The Algarve is not Portugal' – they are referring to several factors which separate this province from the rest of the country. The main difference is the strong Moorish influence to the culture; architecture,

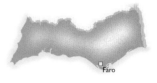

Faro

food, place-names, words in local dialects and even the physical appearance of some Algarvians.

The other main difference is the Mediterranean-type climate which the Algarve enjoys. This, of course, is what has been responsible for the explosion in tourism, turning an agricultural and fishing-based economy into one dependent on holidaymakers from northern Europe, in a single generation.

FARO

Faro is the capital of the Algarve, whose airport, west of the city, is the main gateway for the several million tourists who visit the south coast resorts every year. It is built at the edge of a wide lagoon surrounded by wetlands and salt flats, 10km (6 miles) from a vast beach splintered into sandy islands, some of which emerge and disappear with the tide.

Faro was an important Moorish city which was captured by Afonso III in the dying days of Arab rule in Portugal. It continued to flourish until 1596 when, under Spanish occupation, the town was sacked and burned by the British. In 1755 it was again destroyed – this time by the great earthquake, more famous for having reduced Lisbon to rubble. But despite this,

an attractive walled old
town and a few historic
monuments survive,
warranting a visit into
the heart of the city.
www.cm-faro.pt

🚻 10Y

🛈 Rua da Misericórdia 8

☎ 289 803 604

Capela dos Ossos

Like its better-known counterpart in Évora, the walls of this small,
ghoulish ossuary (chapel of bones) in the crypt of the Igreja do
Carmo are lined with human bones and the grinning skulls of long-
deceased monks, reminding visitors of the certainty of their death.

✉ Largo do Carmo 🕐 Mon–Fri 10–1, 3–5/6, Sat 10–1 👋 Church free;
Chapel inexpensive

a walk around Faro

Start at Jardim Manuel Bivar

These well-tended gardens look out across the harbour and are the only part of town where there is some sense of peace and open space as seabirds call and halyards clink on masts.

> *From the south end of the gardens, enter the old town through the stone arch next to the Turismo. This is the 18th-century Arco da Vila, with its statue of Thomas Aquinas. A short walk along the Rua do Municipo leads into the Largo da Sé (Cathedral Square) and the Sé itself (▶ 170).*

> *Cross the Praça Afonso and leave the old town through the Arco do Repouso, turning left*

onto Rua Manuel Francisco, then right at the crossroads onto Rua Santo António, the main shopping street and just before at the Praça da Liberdade, onto Rua de Portugal. Adjacent to the end of this road is a white-fronted building housing the Teatro Lethes.

Inside the former Jesuit college of Santiago Maior, now the Teatro Lethes, is a chapel converted into a tiny replica of La Scala, Milan's famous opera house. The building stages varied art and other exhibitions.

Cross the Largo das Mouras Velhas and turn right up Rua do Sol, then left, crossing Rua do Alportel into Largo do Poço, which leads into Largo do Carmo.

In the middle of Largo do Carmo stands the Igreja do Carmo, a Carmelite church, whose alluring, if macabre, feature is the Capela dos Ossos (► 167).

Return to the Largo do Poço, and follow the Rua Alistão Vardim as far as Rua 1 de Maio. Turn right here, rejoining the harbour at Praça Francisco Gomes, at the north end of Jardim Manuel Bivar. Walk round the north of the harbour, ending at the Museu Marítimo (► 170).

Distance 3km (2 miles)
Time 2–4 hours, depending on stops
Start point Jardim Manuel Bivar
End point Museu Marítimo
Lunch Dois Irmãos (€€€) ✉ Largo Terreiro do Bispo ☎ 289 823337

Museu Marítimo

The Maritime Museum, housed in the harbour master's office on the seafront, is dedicated to the industry on which Faro's prosperity has depended for centuries – fishing. Models of numerous vessels demonstrate the evolution of the fishing boats and have been re-created with infinite care and detail. Rooms full of other fishing equipment are also on display, including crab and cuttlefish traps and harpoons for spearing shark and tuna.

✉ Rua Comunidade Lusiada ☎ 289 894 990 🕔 Mon–Fri 9–12, 2:30–4. Closed public hols 🖐 Inexpensive

Sé

Faro's cathedral is a jumbled mixture of Gothic, Renaissance and baroque of no great architectural distinction. However, the 17th- and 18th-century *azulejos* in the side chapels on both sides of the nave are worth seeing. The darkened interior can also be deliciously cool on a hot day.

✉ Largo da Sé 🕔 Mon–Sat 10–12:30, 1:30–5. Sun open only during services 🖐 Inexpensive

More to see in the Algarve

ALBUFEIRA

Despite tourist development, Albufeira still
retains some of its original quaint charm. There
are cobbled streets and whitewashed cottages
squatting at the feet of apartment blocks;
hidden away are two simple, rather lovely, old
churches – Capela de Misericórdia (Chapel of
Mercy) and the Igreja de São Sebastião (Church
of Saint Sebastian); and down on the beach
there are still fishermen who draw their gaily
painted wooden boats up onto the sand to sell
their catches.

www.cm-albufeira.pt

✚ 10Y ⊠ 39km (24 miles) west of Faro

ℹ Rua 5 de Outubro ☎ 289 585 279

ALMANCIL

Almancil is best known as a service town to
two of the Algarve's most luxurious resorts,
Vale do Lobo, 4km (2.5 miles) to the south,
and Quinta do Lago just beyond. Both resorts
boast several five-star hotels and country clubs,
designer shops, beautiful beaches and some
of tthe most expensive golfing in the region.

   The town itself has little for the visitor, apart
from the small chapel of São Lourenço on its
eastern outskirts. The hand-painted blue-and-
white tiles covering both walls and ceiling
depict the life of St Lawrence and are
considered to be one of Portugal's finest
displays.

✚ 10Y ⊠ 12km (7.5 miles) northwest of Faro

ALTE

Alte is perhaps one of the Algarve's most attractive, traditional, whitewashed villages. Despite its frequent visits by bus-tours from the coast and local day-trippers on the weekend, the village is well maintained and offers some great photo opportunities among its tranquil winding streets.

Though much adapted in the 16th and 18th centuries, the village church originates from the 13th century and contains some interesting polychrome tiles brought from Seville in the 16th century, a fine Manueline doorway and some intricate woodwork. A few minutes outside town are the village springs, Fonte Grande and Fonte Pequena, where shady tables make a good spot for a picnic lunch.

✚ 10Y

CABO DE SÃO VICENTE

Best places to see, pages 40–41.

LAGOS

History-packed Lagos is among the most attractive of the Algarve's coastal towns. To a large extent it has survived the advent of

tourism with its charm intact, because most of the development has been outside the town. In Praça Infante Dom Henrique there is a large bronze statue of Henry the Navigator holding his sextant and gazing out to sea. Leading off from the square are cobbled, pedestrianized streets lined with cafés, bars and restaurants where you can sit and eat or drink *al fresco* while enjoying the cheerful ambience.

www.cm-lagos.pt

✚ 9Y ✉ 16km (10 miles) west of Portimão

🛈 Rua D Vasco da Gama ☎ 282 763 031

a drive around western Algarve

Start from Lagos. Take the 125 westwards, signposted Sagres (▶ 178). Continue 6km (4 miles) along the cliff-top road, to Cabo de São Vicente (▶ 40–41). Return to the road junction just above Sagres, and take the 268 northwards, signposted to Vila do Bispo. Go into the village and take the narrow road behind the town stadium signposted Praia do Castelejo.

The huge beach of Praia do Castelejo is backed by high cliffs and gets few visitors. The sea is rough and often cold, tempting only a few dedicated surfers. However, it is an excellent place to appreciate the raw beauty of the western Algarve, and to lunch in the beach café.

Return to Vila do Bispo, and continue north on the 268 to Aljezur.

Elsewhere in Europe, the old town of Aljezur, topped by a ruined castle, might have a turnstile, official guide and ice-cream stand. But climb to the castle for wonderful views over the west coast, and you will probably have the place to yourself.

From Aljezur, take the 267 inland (eastwards), into the gentle green Monchique hills, to the town of Monchique (➤ 176–177). Four kilometres (2.5 miles) south of Monchique, just off the 268, is the pretty spa town of Caldas de Monchique.

Caldas de Monchique is where the ubiquitous Monchique mineral water comes from. On the main square are some fine old façades belonging to the era of 19th-century gentility when the spa was popular with wealthy Spaniards. Some delightful trails lead off into the woods, from just behind the square.

The 268 continues south, through orchards and citrus groves, rejoining the 125 west of Portimão. Turn right to return to Lagos.

Distance 165km (102 miles)
Time 4–6 hours including stops
Start/end point Lagos ✚ 9Y
Lunch Praia do Castelejo beach café (€)

MONCHIQUE

The best day to visit the main town of the Monchique hills is the second Friday of every month, when there is a large market with farmers from a wide area bringing their produce for sale, as well as ceramics and handicrafts.

Foia, the highest peak in the Algarve (902m/2,960ft), overlooks the town, offering the most sensational views on a clear day. Four kilometres (2.5 miles) south of Monchique are the Caldas de Monchique, a therapeutic spa since Roman times. Enjoy walks in

the countryside around the 19th- and 20th-century complex, which boasts state of the art treatments.

www.cm-monchique.pt

✚ 9X ✉ Monchique is 25km (15.5 miles) north of Portimão

ℹ Largo dos Chorões ☎ 282 911 189

PORTIMÃO

Portimão is surrounded by an ugly urban sprawl, though there are a few points of interest for those who penetrate the centre, such as the Largo Primeiro de Dezembro, and Igreja Matriz. There is excellent shopping on the cobbled walkways between Rua do Comércio and Rua Vasco da Gama.

Seafood is landed fresh each morning at the town quayside and the simple seafood restaurants just off the dock are some of the most atmospheric places on the Algarve to enjoy charcoal grilled sardines.

Portimão's beach is at Praia da Rocha (2km/1.2 miles from town), once the jewel of the coast, magnificently overhung by red sandstone cliffs and pitted with numerous caves. The huge beach of fine sand is strewn with rugged outcrops sculpted by nature into weird formations and backed now by huge hotel complexes.

www.cm-portimao.pt

✚ 9Y ✉ 62km (38 miles) west of Faro

ℹ Avenida Zeca Afonso ☎ 282 470732

SAGRES

The small town where Prince Henry the Navigator set up his famous School of Navigation is out on the very corner of Europe. The scenery is suitably dramatic: solid, bare, windswept bluffs with steps hewn out of them lead down to beaches where the tide washes around in great sweeps, while gulls hover high above.

www.sagres.net

➕ 8Y ✉ 33km (20 miles) west of Lagos

ℹ Rua Comandante Matoso ☎ 282 624 873

SILVES

Silves was the old Moorish capital of the Algarve, recaptured by Christian forces in 1249. It was an Atlantic port until the River Arade silted up. The aura of the Moors lives on, as you will discover if you take a walk round the old, restored castle walls. Also worth seeing is the 13th-century Sé de Santa Maria (Cathedral), and the **Museum of Archaeology,** which puts the town's history into context.

www.cm-silves.pt

➕ 9Y ✉ 7km (4 miles) northeast of Portimão

ℹ Rua 25 de Abril 9 ☎ 282 442 255

Museum of Archaeology

✉ Rua das Portas de Loulé ☎ 282 444832 🕐 Mon–Sat 9–6

✋ Inexpensive

TAVIRA

Best places to see, pages 52–53.

VILAMOURA

The most extensive tourist complex in Portugal. Vilamoura started off as a development of posh villas around a superb golf course; now there are four 18-hole courses and a wide range of villas, apartments and hotels. Vilamoura has neither the exclusive air of Vale de Lobo nor the seediness of Albufeira, although elements of each can be found in the sharply contrasting 'villages' which make up the resort. The sports facilities are the best in the Algarve; as well as golf courses, there are more than 50 tennis courts and all kinds of watersports around a huge marina with over 1,000 berths.

www.vilamoura.net

✚ 10Y ✉ 26km (16 miles) west of Faro

HOTELS

ALBUFEIRA
Sheraton Algarve (€€€)

A complete resort (also known as Pinecliffs), east of Albufeira, with golf course, spa, watersports and other attractions.

✉ Pinhal do Concelho ☎ 289 500 102; www.pinecliffs.com

FARO
Hotel Eva (€€–€€€)

Faro's top hotel, with rooms overlooking the harbour and sea.

✉ Avenida da Republica ☎ 289 803 354

LAGOS
Casa da Moura (€€–€€€)

Set inside medieval town walls with North African-influenced interiors. Apartments have small kitchenettes. Terrace and pool.

✉ Rua Cardeal Neto 10 ☎ 282 770 730; www.casadamoura.com

MONCHIQUE
Termas de Monchique (€€)

Accommodation at the thermal spa, from self-catering apartments to a pension or inn. Spa treatments charged separately.

✉ Caldas de Monchique ☎ 282 910 910; www.monchiquetermas.com

PORTIMÃO
Penina (€€€)

A very famous golf hotel. It now belongs the Meridien group.

✉ PO Box 146 – between Portimão and Lagos ☎ 282 420 200; www.lemeridien.com

PRAIA DA ROCHA
Hotel Oriental (€€–€€€)

This luxurious, beautifully designed small hotel, with its distinctive oriental touches, sits overlooking the beach at Praia da Rocha.

✉ Avenida Tomás Cabreira ☎ 282 480800; www.tdhotels.pt

SAGRES
Pousada do Infante (€€–€€€)
Pousada with a sensational location on the bluffs of Sagres.
✉ 8650-385 Sagres ☎ 282 620 240; www.pousadas.pt

SILVES
Hotel Colina dos Mouros (€–€€)
Modern Moorish-style hotel across the valley with views of Silves.
✉ Pocinho Santo, 8301 Silves ☎ 282 440 420; www.colinaresorts.8k.com

TAVIRA
Vila Galé Albacora (€€–€€€)
Beautiful low-level hacienda-style hotel located on the river outside
Tavira. An excellent place to relax, with pools, spa and gym.
✉ Quatro Águas ☎ 281 380 800; www.vilagale.pt

RESTAURANTS

ALBUFEIRA
Atrium (€€)
Good fish, international cuisine and an excellent wine list.
✉ Rua 5 de Outubro 2 ☎ 289 515 755

Tasca do Viegas (€€)
The closest thing in Albufeira to a typically Portuguese restaurant.
✉ Cais Herculano 2 ☎ 289 514087 🕐 Closed Sun

ALMANCIL
São Gabriel (€€€)
One of a few restaurants in this select area of the Algarve to have
earned a Michelin star. International menu. Bookings essential.
✉ Quinto do Lago ☎ 289 394 521 🕐 Closed lunch and Mon

BURGAU
Beach Bar (€€)
Excellent grilled sardines and other fish; terrace on the beach.
✉ Burgau (west of Lagos) ☎ 282 697 553 🕐 Closed Mon out of season

CARRAPATEIRA
Sitio do Forno (€€)
Panoramic views of Amado beach and the Atlantic from the cliff-side terrace, and excellent fresh fish.

✉ Praia do Amado ☎ 963 558 404 ⊙ Closed Mon

FARO
A Taska (€)
An excellent, traditional tavern, of a kind that is hard to find in the Algarve.

✉ Rua do Alportel 38 ☎ 289 824 739 ⊙ Closed Sun

Cidade Velha (€€)
Pleasant, cosy restaurant that is well located in Faro's old town. The menu offers international and traditional southern cuisine.

✉ Rua Domingo Guieiro 19 ☎ 289 827 145

Dois Irmãos (€€)
Generally considered to be one of Faro's best haunts, serving a range of excellent fish and seafood dishes.

✉ Largo Terreiro do Bispo 13–15 ☎ 289 823 337

Mesa dos Mouros (€€)
Pretty converted house with a small terrace and cosy dining room.

✉ Largo da Sé ☎ 289 878 873 ⊙ Closed Sat lunch and Sun

LAGOS
Dom Sebastião (€€)
Top-notch restaurant, serving a wide range of international and southern Portuguese dishes. Book ahead, especially in summer.

✉ Rua 25 de Abril 20–22 ☎ 282 780 480

MONCHIQUE
Restaurant Bica-Boca (€€)
One of Western Algarve's best restaurants serving Portuguese and international dishes. Just north of town on the N266 Lisbon road.

✉ Estrada de Lisboa ☎ 282 912 271

PRAIA DE LUZ
Fortaleza da Luz (€€)
Portuguese dishes and fresh fish in the 16th-century fortress.

✉ Rua da Igreja 3 ☎ 282 789 926 🕓 Closed mid-Nov to mid-Dec

SAGRES
A Tasca (€€)
Fresh fish and enchanting views of the harbour.

✉ Praia da Baleeira ☎ 282 624 177 🕓 Closed Wed

SILVES
Café Ingles (€€)
Elegant 1920s mansion with a large terrace under the shadow of Silves cathedral. Good Portuguese and international snacks.

✉ Escadas do Castello II ☎ 282 442 585

TAVIRA
Imperial (€€)
Well known for its big, fresh, meaty fish steaks.

✉ Rua José Pires Padinha 22 ☎ 281 322 306 🕓 Closed Wed and Jan

SHOPPING

GLASS, PORCELAIN AND CERAMICS
Casa Algarve
One of the best of many local ceramics shops along this stretch of road, with an endless array of artefacts.

✉ On the north side of the main N125, Porches ☎ 282 352 682

Estudio Destra
Ceramic artist Roger Metcalfe produces an excellent range of *azulejo* murals in modern styles and also undertakes commissions.

✉ Largo Jeronimo Osorio, Silves ☎ 282 442 933

O Aquario
A very stylish shop selling a selection of Atlantis crystal glass, Vista Alegre porcelain and other high quality products.

✉ Rua Vasco da Gama 42–46, Portimão ☎ 282 426 673

Porches Pottery

The Algarve's most famous ceramics centre, which features many *avante-garde* creations, as well as traditional Algarvian pottery.

✉ On the south side of the N125, Porches ☎ 282 352 858

HANDICRAFTS AND SOUVENIRS

A Mó

Large selection of traditional Algarve pottery and souvenirs.

✉ Located on the Cabo San Vincente road, Sagres

Bazar-Miriamis

A great range of handicrafts and ceramics of all kinds, from the Algarve and elsewhere in Portugal. Shipment of goods can be arranged.

✉ Largo do Dique 11, Portimão ☎ 282 423 510

Casa dos Arcos

Monchique's speciality is simple, folding wooden chairs. They are easily transportable and this is the place to buy some of the best.

✉ Rua Auguste Gulbenkian, Monchique ☎ 282 911 071

Portas do Castelo

Excellent range of modern cork products plus other *artesanato*.

✉ Praça da República 1–3, Tavira ☎ 281 325 984

MARKET

Farmers from a wide area bring their produce here, as well as ceramics and handicrafts aimed principally at tourists from the coastal resorts.

✉ Monchique ⏰ Third Fri of every month

WINE

Pousada Porto

Reputed to be the best wine shop in Faro, including an excellent selection of Alentejo wines.

✉ Rua do Bocage 50, Faro

ENTERTAINMENT

CASINOS

Casino da Vilamoura

✉ Vilamoura, Quarteira ☎ 289 310 000; www.solverde.pt

DISCOS AND NIGHTCLUBS

Capitulo V

Chill out at this fashionable nightspot where you can rub shoulders with celebrities.

✉ Ed. Borda de Agua, Praia de Oura, Albufeira; www.capitulov.com

Kadoc

Discotheque and live music venue in one. Excellent guest DJs throughout the year.

✉ Estrada Vilamoura Bolequeime, Vilamoura

Kathedral Nightclub

Mixed music with theme nights, best during the summer.

✉ Avenida Tomás Cabreira, Praia da Rocha

Kiss

Wild and popular club, always packed to the gunnels from midnight to 4am in summer.

✉ Areisa de São João, Albufeira

Liberto's

Liberto's styles itself as an up-market disco bar.

✉ Avenida Sá Carneiro, Areias de São João, Apartado 553, Albufeira

Locomia

One of the most trendy discos around found on Santa Eulália beach.

✉ Praia de Santa Eulália, Albufeira

Index

Acknowledgements

The Automobile Association would like to thank the following photographers, companies and picture libraries for their assistance in the preparation of this book.
Abbreviations for the picture credits are as follows – (t) top; (b) bottom; (c) centre; (l) left; (r) right; (AA) AA World Travel Library.

4l View from the top of the Monument to the Discoveries, AA/A Kouprianoff; **4c** Molceiros boats, AA/A Mockford & N Bonetti; **4r** Fisherman in Tavira, AA/C Jones; **5l** Rio Cavado, AA/A Mockford & N Bonetti; **5r** Coimbra, AA/A Kouprianoff; **6/7** View from the Monument to the Discoveries, AA/A Kouprianoff; **8/9** Fisherman's pots, AA/C Jones; **10c** Sorting shrimp, AA/A Mockford & N Bonetti; **10bl** Sheep in meadow, AA/A Mockford & N Bonetti; **10br** Village of Monsaraz, AA/J Edmanson; **10/1t** Colourful textiles, AA/M Chaplow; **10/1c** Newspaper stand, AA/A Mockford & N Bonetti; **10/1b** Marvão, AA/A Kouprianoff; **11tr** Tavira, AA/C Jones; **11cr** Figueira da Foz, AA/A Kouprianoff; **11br** Religious souvenirs, AA/A Kouprianoff; **12bl** Tomatoes, AA/A Kouprianoff; **12br** Fish stall, AA/T Harris; **12/3t** Marzipan sweets, AA/C Jones; **12/3c** Watermelons, AA/J Edmanson; **12/3b** Piri piri chicken, AA/C Jones; **13tl** Café sign, AA/A Mockford & N Bonetti; **13tr** Peppers for sale, AA/C Jones; **13br** Chestnuts for sale, AA/C Jones; **14** Produce, AA/A Mockford & N Bonetti; **14/5t** Grapes, AA/A Kouprianoff; **14/5b** Barrels of port, AA/T Harris; **15tr** Glasses of port, AA/T Harris; **15cr** Honey pots, AA/C Jones; **15br** Serpa, AA/J Edmanson; **16** Cork trees, AA/P Wilson; **16/7** Torre de Belém, AA/T Harris; **17t** Sardines, AA/M Birkitt; **17c** Tram, AA/A Kouprianoff; **17b** Cabo de São Vicente lighthouse, AA/M Chaplow; **18** Market, AA/A Mockford & N Bonetti; **18/9t** Port, AA/T Harris; **18/9b** Silves, AA/J Edmanson; **20/1** Molceiros boats, AA/A Mockford & N Bonetti; **25** Festival of Tabuleiros, AA/P Wilson; **27** Bus, AA/A Mockford & N Bonetti; **28** Sign, AA/A Mockford & N Bonetti; **30** Postbox, AA/ C Jones; **31** Telephone, AA/A Mockford & N Bonetti; **34/5** Fisherman, AA/C Jones; **36/7** Alcobaça, AA/A Kouprianoff; **37** Alcobaça, AA/A Kouprianoff; **38t** Batalha Abbey, AA/A Kouprianoff; **38b** Capela do Fundador, Batalha, AA/A Kouprianoff; **39** Batalha Abbey, AA/A Kouprianoff; **40** Cabo de São Vicente, AA/M Chaplow; **40/1** Cabo de São Vicente, AA/A Mockford & N Bonetti; **42** Rolling hills near Monsaraz, AA/A Kouprianoff; **42/3** Monsaraz, AA/A Kouprianoff; **44/5t** Mosteiro dos Jerónimos, AA/A Kouprianoff; **44/5b** Mosteiro dos Jerónimos, AA/A Kouprianoff; **46** Mosque lamp at the Museu Calouste Gulbenkian, AA/A Kouprianoff; **47** Gardens at the Museu Calouste Gulbenkian, AA/A Kouprianoff; **48** Óbidos, AA/P Wilson; **48/9t** Óbidos, AA/A Kouprianoff; **48/9b** Óbidos, AA/A Kouprianoff; **50** Serra da Estrela, AA/T Harris; **51** Serra da Estrela, AA/T Harris; **52** Tavira, AA/C Jones; **53** Tavira, AA/C Jones; **54/5** Vila Nova de Gaia, AA/A Mockford & N Bonetti; **55** Bottle of Sandeman vintage port, AA/A Mockford & N Bonetti; **56/7** Peneda-Gerês National Park, AA/A Mockford & N Bonetti; **58/9** Café, AA/A Kouprianoff; **60/1** Sailing trip, AA/A Kouprianoff; **62/3** Solar de Mateus, AA/T Harris; **65** Cockerel, AA/A Mockford & N Bonetti; **66/7** Ilha de Tavira, AA/A Kouprianoff; **69** Zoomarine, AA/C Jones; **70/1** Santa Luzia Basilica, AA/P Wilson; **72** Golf course, AA/C Jones; **75** Marvão, AA/A Kouprianoff; **76** Peneda-Gerês National Park, AA/T Harris; **78/9** View of Coimbra, AA/A Kouprianoff; **80** Molceiros boats, AA/A Mockford & N Bonetti; **82** Lady reading in Porto, AA/A Mockford & N Bonetti; **83t** Port lodges of Gaia, AA/A Mockford & N Bonetti; **83b** Fundação Serralves, AA/T Harris; **84** Ribeira area of Porto, AA/T Harris; **84/5** The Dom Luis Bridge, AA/P Wilson; **85** Cais da Ribeira, AA/A Mockford & N Bonetti; **86** Igreja de São Francisco, Kevin George/Alamy; **86/7** Museu de Soares dos Reis, Carlos Monteiro, Instituto Portugues de Museus; **88** Sé in Porto, AA/A Kouprianoff; **89** Amarante, AA/A Mockford & N Bonetti; **90/1** Aveiro, AA/A Mockford & N Bonetti; **91** Festa das Cruzes, AA/P Wilson; **92t** Braga, AA/A Mockford & N Bonetti; **92b** Braga cathedral, AA/P Wilson; **93** Bom Jesus sanctuary, AA/ A Kouprianoff; **94** Bragança, AA/A Mockford & N Bonetti; **95** Bragança, AA/A Mockford & N Bonetti; **96/7t** University buildings in Coimbra, AA; **96/7b** University buildings in Coimbra, AA; **98** Paço dos Duques, AA/A Mockford & N Bonetti; **98/9** Figueira da Foz, AA/A Kouprianoff; **99** Guimarães, AA/A Mockford & N Bonetti; **100t** Buçaco Palace Hotel, AA/A Mockford & N Bonetti; **100b** Buçaco Palace Hotel, AA/A Mockford & N Bonetti; **101** Vintage car museum in Caramulo, AA/P Wilson; **102/3** View from Santa Luzia, AA/P Wilson; **104** Viseu, AA; **113** View from Castelo de São Jorge, AA/A Kouprianoff; **114** Parque das Nações, Lisbon, AA/A Mockford & N Bonetti; **115** Parque das Nações, Lisbon, AA/A Mockford & N Bonetti; **116** Shoeshine, AA/A Mockford & N Bonetti; **116/7** Tiles on building near Baixa, AA/A Kouprianoff; **117** Sculpture in Baixa, AA/A Mockford & N Bonetti; **118/9** Castelo de São Jorge, AA/T Harris; **119** Museu da Marinha, AA/A Kouprianoff; **120** Oceanario, AA/T Harris; **120/1** Museu Nacional dos Coches, AA/A Kouprianoff; **122** Rossio Square, AA/T Harris; **122/3** Rossio Square, AA/T Harris; **124/5** Sé, Lisbon, AA/A Mockford & N Bonetti; **125** Torre de Belém, AA/P Wilson; **126** Cascais, AA/A Mockford & N Bonetti; **126/7** Estoril, AA/A Mockford & N Bonetti; **128** Sesimbra, AA/P Wilson; **128/9** Sesimbra, AA/A Mockford & N Bonetti; **129** Sesimbra, AA/A Mockford & N Bonetti; **130** Belltower in Fatima, AA/A Mockford & N Bonetti; **130/1** Azulejos in Leiria, AA; **132** Handicrafts in Sintra, AA/A Mockford & N Bonetti; **132/3** Sintra, AA/T Harris; **134** Tomar, AA/T Harris; **143** Convento da Nossa Senhora de Conceição, AA/M Birkitt; **144** Shop in Évora, AA/A Mockford & N Bonetti; **145** Chapel of Bones in Évora, AA/P Wilson; **146** Shops in Évora, AA/A Mockford & N Bonetti; **147** Praça do Giraldo, AA/A Mockford & N Bonetti; **148/9** Cathedral in Évora, J Edmanson; **150** Templo Romano, AA/A Kouprianoff; **151l** Convento da Nossa Senhora de Conceição, AA/M Birkitt; **151r** Convento da Nossa Senhora de Conceição, AA/A Kouprianoff; **152** Elvas, AA/J Edmanson; **152/3** Estremoz, AA; **154** Serpa, AA/J Edmanson; **154/5** Mertola, AA/A Kouprianoff; **155** Mertola, AA/M Birkitt; **156** Marvao, AA/A Kouprianoff; **156/7** Paco Ducal, AA/A Mockford & N Bonetti; **165** Portimao, AA/C Jones; **166** Faro, AA/C Jones; **166/7** Fisherman, AA/C Jones; **167** Igreja do Carmo, AA/A Kouprianoff; **168** Mosaic, AA/C Jones; **168/9** Arco de Villa, AA/C Jones; **169** Cathedral Square, AA/C Jones; **170** Sé, AA/J Edmanson; **170/1** Albufeira, AA/A Kouprianoff; **172/3** Alte, AA/A Mockford & N Bonetti; **173** Lagos, AA/A Mockford & N Bonetti; **174/5** Aljezur, AA/M Chaplow; **175** Aljezur, AA/M Chaplow; **176/7** Monchique, AA/J Edmanson; **177** Sardines, AA/C Jones; **178t** Fisherman, AA/C Jones; **178b** Silves, AA/M Chaplow; **178/9** Vilamoura, AA/C Jones.

Every effort has been made to trace the copyright holders, and we apologise in advance for any accidental errors. We would be happy to apply the corrections in the following edition of this publication.

Sight Locator Index

This index relates to the maps on the covers. We have given map references to the main sights in the book. Grid references in italics indicate sights featured on the town plan. Some sights within towns may not be plotted on the maps.

Questionnaire

Dear Traveler

Your comments, opinions and recommendations are very important to us.
So please help us to improve our travel guides by taking a few minutes to
complete this simple questionnaire.

Send to: Essential Guides,
MailStop 64, 1000 AAA Drive, Heathrow, FL 32746–5063

Your recommendations...

We always encourage readers' recommendations for restaurants, nightlife
or shopping – if your recommendation is added to the next edition of the
guide, we will send you a FREE AAA Essential Guide of your choice.
Please state below the establishment name, location and your reasons for
recommending it.

_____

_____

_____

_____

_____

Please send me AAA Essential _____

About this guide...

Which title did you buy?

_____ **AAA Essential**

Where did you buy it? _____

When? m m / y y

Why did you choose a AAA Essential Guide? _____

_____

_____

Did this guide meet with your expectations?

Exceeded ☐   Met all ☐   Met most ☐   Fell below ☐

Please give your reasons _____

_____

_____

continued on next page...

Were there any aspects of this guide that you particularly liked? _____

_____

_____

_____

_____

_____

Is there anything we could have done better? _____

_____

_____

_____

_____

_____

About you...
Name (Mr/Mrs/Ms) _____

Address _____

_____ **Zip** _____

Daytime tel nos. _____

Which age group are you in?
Under 25 ☐   25–34 ☐   35–44 ☐   45–54 ☐   55–64 ☐   65+ ☐

How many trips do you make a year?
Less than one ☐   One ☐   Two ☐   Three or more ☐

Are you a AAA member?   Yes ☐   No ☐

Name of AAA club _____

About your trip
When did you book? m m / y y   **When did you travel?** m m / y y

How long did you stay? _____

Was it for business or leisure? _____

Did you buy any other travel guides for your trip?   Yes ☐   No ☐

If yes, which ones? _____

Thank you for taking the time to complete this questionnaire.